Using the
Personal Computer for
Offensive Football Scouting:

THE NEW COMPETITIVE EDGE

ALAN B. HATFIELD
and
CHARLES S. FRAZIER

Parker Publishing Co., Inc.   ·   West Nyack, New York

This book is dedicated to those in the coaching profession
who spend their time scouting the games, breaking down
the films, attending the clinics, and using the hours to
improve their expertise in the great game of football.

© 1985 *by*

Parker Publishing Company, Inc.
West Nyack, New York

Library of Congress Cataloging in Publication Data

Hatfield, Alan B.
Using the personal computer for offensive scouting.

Includes index.
1. Football—Scouting—Data processing.   2. Football—
Coaching—Data processing.   I. Frazier, Charles S.,
II. Title.
GV953.4.H37 1985   796.332′2′02854   84–27680

ISBN 0-13-939570-9

Printed in the United States of America

WHAT THIS BOOK HAS TO OFFER

Chapter 1 is a discussion of the six pieces of equipment that comprise a complete personal computer system for computerized scouting. Over 30 terms are defined to help you become computer competent. So that you can choose exactly what you need and get the most for your money, *before* you buy, over 50 guidelines for evaluating equipment have been included.

Chapters 2 and 3 present an overview of how to organize your computerized scouting system. They begin by discussing eight important forms included in a complete scouting manual, and six opportunities for training your scouts. Four different schedules, with one capable of keeping track of 14 separate items, are covered. Twelve guidelines are presented to keep your computerized scouting system running smoothly throughout the season.

In Chapters 4, 5, and 6 a compact, efficient, and flexible method is suggested for gathering the scouting data for your personal computer at the game site or later from film breakdown. By using four sample plays from an actual game, the when, what, and how aspects of computerized scouting are covered. Included are: the four different times when data are gathered, what the ten pieces of information with ten optional items actually are, and how each item is recorded to make it compatible with the personal computer. An easy-to-use system for recording up to 100 formations, motions, and shifts for today's multiple offenses is given. The recording of ten different points of attack with 40 different blocking schemes and ten different passing zones with over 80 different receiver routes is itemized. Also presented is a discussion of the treatment of special situations such as recording 11 different option plays or six different call blocking schemes for the same play.

The keystroke by keystroke sequence of typing the data on the keyboard, entering it in the computer's memory, and saving it for permanent use on an initialized diskette are covered, with over ten sample computer displays included. Self-check systems and the four common mistakes which all personal computer users make are covered. A discussion of how to quickly correct these errors is presented. Making back-up copies of all your work is also discussed.

Chapters 7 and 8 present an interpretation of the information that the computer presents with an emphasis on the four sample plays previously discussed. Included are the seven breakdown areas and four charts available for determining your opponent's offensive tendencies. Over 30 actual computer printouts presenting almost 70 calculated categories are used to track over 20 actual tendencies for the four sample plays. *How not to use the printouts* is also discussed.

In Chapters 9 and 10 the opponent's tendencies are implemented as a game plan takes shape. The 11 sections of a complete game plan folder and who's responsible for each section are reviewed. Three different tables are included. Eighteen diagrams supplement this section. A list of the eight parts of the player's report is included. Four different game week practice schedules and the reasons why each practice should be set up differently are explained.

The entire system is employed in a discussion of game day. Seventeen specific responsibilities of four different coaches are listed in the press box-to-sideline procedures. Also included is a discussion of three important game charts and the most efficient use of the most critical time during a game—halftime. The use of a personal computer is brought full circle as the four charts and three printouts for the postgame analysis are mentioned. Here, the performances of your opponent and your players are analyzed, and the decisions made by you and your coaches are evaluated.

In the final chapter, 13 more terms are defined to help you decide which football scouting computer program is best for your needs. Information on the current, applicable programs offered by 32 suppliers is given in six different areas. To further guide your choice, 23 specific considerations are listed to make sure that you get exactly what you want at a price you can afford.

The football scouting section of this book concludes with a listing of 32 suppliers and 38 programs, takes a look at the future of computer application, issues two challenges directed at coaches wishing to maintain the new competitive edge, and adds some final comments for all coaches to consider.

Since most coaches, especially at the high school level, are involved in other sports, have athletic administrative responsibilities, or run off-season programs, over 80 software packages in 20 different areas from 30 suppliers are included in the Athletic Software Directory.

Indexed and cross-referenced by company, subject, and description, this directory may be used by all athletic coaches.

GAINING THE NEW COMPETITIVE EDGE

There is a new competitive edge beginning to emerge in football, and it is occurring all the way down to the high school level. That competitive edge is the use of personal computers in the analysis of football scouting reports. The use of computers is not new to football—that occurred in the late 1960s. The use of personal computers, which made computerized scouting available at all levels, is new. Only since the latter part of the 1970s have reliable, inexpensive, personal computers been available to the general public, and only since the early 1980s have computerized scouting programs become widely advertised and easily attainable across the country.

If you have coached football for very long, you have spent countless hours compiling, summarizing, and analyzing scouting reports. You have wondered if there isn't a better way to gain a competitive edge. Finally, there is a better way.

We have written this book to tell you how, in less than an hour, you can prepare a scouting report of your next opponent. We will show you how this task, which in the past took several coaches many hours to perform, can now be completed more quickly, accurately, and efficiently by a single coach.

After many years of experience scouting football, and after spending many weekends and long hours preparing scouting reports, we decided to take advantage of one of the most revolutionary developments in history—the personal computer.

We discovered that information it would otherwise take hours to compile, may be obtained within minutes with a computer. We discovered that the computer will compile, analyze, summarize, store, and retrieve information and display and print reports; that it will instantly and accurately do just about everything you want done with the information you put into it. Since we compile, analyze, and summarize information to prepare scouting reports, we asked ourselves, why do it manually when there is such a demand on a coach's time during the season? It can literally be done in minutes on a computer.

More surprising, we discovered that computers are easy to learn to operate. They are designed to be run by nontechnical people. No previous experience or knowledge of computers is necessary. There is nothing frightening or magical about computers. The computer is just like any other machine or tool. A fear of computers will soon seem as ridiculous as the initial public fears of automobiles, airplanes, or electricity. Computers will become commonplace, and coaches who become familiar with them now will have a tremendous advantage.

During the space age a major breakthrough occurred in computer technology. The demand for the high standards necessary to send our astronauts into space resulted in the perfection of computer systems. These advancements have led to our present-day microcomputers—the small home or personal computers that are widely advertised. These are the computers that are used in our public schools.

At Klein Forest High School in Houston, Texas, we put these classroom computers to use to more efficiently and effectively scout our opponents. We found an existing football scouting program and, with the aid of a few computer-oriented students, went through the program line for line adapting it to our needs and equipment. Our scouting reports are prepared during weekends, so there is no conflict with the classroom use of the computer. For our scouting needs, our computer does everything we want and has led to a better knowledge of opponents and a more efficient use of practice time. With our computer, one of our coaches is able to enter the full game report in less than half an hour. A task that took several coaches several hours to perform is completed more accurately and efficiently by only one coach using our computer.

Every football coach from the smallest high school team to the professional ranks can greatly benefit from a computerized scouting preparation of a scouting report. A well-prepared scouting report will give any team a competitive edge.

We have written this book to help give you a competitive edge through the use of a computer. When you have finished the book, you should be able to select the proper equipment to implement a computerized scouting system at your school. Whether your athletic department uses a school computer or purchases its own, you will need to know what kind of equipment to select. Microcomputers can be purchased at affordable prices in the range of almost any athletic department budget.

Necessary guidelines will be given to train and organize your staff more efficiently to make the most of their skills as scouts, planners of game strategy, on-the-field coaches, and press box spotters. Included is important information on collecting data at the game site and from game films, and on compiling and storing the data. Another essential area covered is interpretation of the information collected.

Breaking down your opponent's tendencies and developing a game plan will be shown. All of our material is accompanied by charts, forms, coding keys, and examples. How to organize scouting material for the game day will be explained.

You will be able to choose just the right computer program to get the most out of your carefully selected equipment and highly organized staff. There is a good selection of football scouting programs on the market today. As a result of selecting a good program, you will be able to spend your weekends devising a game plan to beat your opponents rather than shuffling scouting materials.

This book has been written so that you can skip around and not have to read straight through. As a first step, you may want to read the chapters on the organization and implementation of a typical computerized scouting system and its use in game plan preparation. Then you may want to read the chapter on computer programs that are already available. Once you have convinced yourself of the value of a computerized scouting system, read the first chapter on the selection of the right computer for your school. Even if you already have a computerized system and know the mechanics of computerized scouting, you should be alert for ways to improve your methods.

You needn't know much about automotive mechanics to drive a car, and you needn't know much about computer electronics to operate a computer. Some computer basics will be covered, however, so that the equipment won't be quite so mysterious. There will be a brief discussion of the languages that make people and computers conversant. The invention of these languages made computers easily accessible to the large number of people who had no previous contact with them. When you have finished this book, you will be able to put the new competitive edge to work for your school.

Although one of the most effective uses of the computer is offensive football scouting, there are many other areas in which the computer can be effectively utilized in athletics today. As a matter of fact, coaches and athletic directors find that the more they use the computer, the more uses they can find for the computer. The possibilities are almost limitless. Because this is such an important subject for athletic administrators and coaches of all sports, we have included Appendix A to discuss these other uses of the computer in athletics.

Also, if you are like most coaches you probably do not know where to find software for athletic uses, or even what software is available for athletic uses. In Appendix B we have provided you with an Athletic Software Directory. It is the most accurate and comprehensive list of athletic software available to coaches today. It will aid you in locating the latest athletic software. The question most often asked by coaches about the computer is, "What can I do with it?" This directory goes a long way toward answering this question. Just pick a subject area, look it up in the directory and you will probably find a number of sources for the software along with a brief description of what the program will do for you.

To be competitive today, coaches must come to grips with the computer. You can take advantage of this revolutionary development through study, knowledge, common sense, and practice. Knowledge and use of the computer can help you work better and faster—and will give you the new competitive edge.

ACKNOWLEDGMENTS

To W. T. for his success over 44 years of coaching and administration, which is a constant inspiration.

To Deo for her love and support.

To Camille for typing the manuscript and providing the love that makes life worthwhile.

To Lavonne for her love and patience.

To Ray Moss, Jack Jones, Bob Hoffman, Leonard Bryant, and Bill Kuykendahl for their early guidance.

To Bill Reichow for the opportunity to learn the sport from both sides of the ball.

To Clay Cooper whose office door is always open.

To Rich Davies for the invaluable scouting experience.

To Tommy Ward for the challenge to coach in Texas.

To Jim McGuire for the original program.

To Eddie Knipfer for his help in translating the program.

To George Wheeler for his answers to countless questions.

To all the players at Mizzou, Rock Bridge, Cy-Fair, and Klein Forest whose progress is the true reward in coaching.

If you have the Will To Prepare,
the Will to Win takes care of itself.

Charles (Bud) Wilkinson

Contents

CHAPTER **1**

CHOOSING YOUR HARDWARE

In this chapter we are going to give you all the information that you as a buyer will need to research the latest in personal computer hardware. We don't expect to make you an electronics expert, but we will give you enough information to confidently walk into a computer store armed with all the knowledge and all the questions necessary to make an intelligent decision within your budget on the purchase of a personal computer.

BECOMING COMPUTER LITERATE

Computer hardware includes the computer and its input-output devices such as the keyboard, the disk drive, the monitor, and the printer. All of these are electronic or mechanical devices. The personal computer system consists of a typewriter-style keyboard which includes the electronic circuitry, a disk drive with diskette for program storage and input, a TV or video monitor for simultaneous readout, and a printer with paper for production of a hard copy or printed copy (Photo 1-1). At the heart of the system is the computer itself, usually a low box with a keyboard that looks something like an electric typewriter, or a box attached to the keyboard by a cord. The computer alone can not communicate with the outside world. Its systems remain useless until two important components are added: a device through which a user can tell the computer what to do; and a device for communication of the computed results. In short, a computer needs data fed in (input), so it can send data out (output).

1

1-1   Monitor, Keyboard, Disk Drive

For entering information into the computer, the two most common devices are the keyboard and the disk drive. The keyboard lets you enter any information you choose, but if you had to send the computer every set of instructions via the keyboard, you would spend all your time typing and very little time using the information the computer gives back. You need a way to send previously written instructions to the computer at more computerlike speeds. The disk drive performs this input function. This little machine, attached to or built into the computer, reads the information stored on a diskette or floppy disk, a circular plastic disk that looks like a small, flexible 45 rpm record in a cardboard or vinyl jacket. The disk drive then feeds the information to the computer in seconds (Photos 1-2, 1-3, 1-4).

Personal computers send out information in three ways. The first is through a small TV or video monitor. Plugged into the monitor, a computer can instantly display numbers, words, and pictures on the screen. The second way is through the disk drive, which can write information on the diskette as well as receive instructions. The computer sends its data to the disk drive, which quickly records the information on the diskette. Although almost all computer attachments can be classified as either input or output devices, the disk drive is both an input and output device. The third way that a computer delivers information is through a printer attached to the computer. The printer lets you make hard or printed copies of all your work.

1-2   Printer

1-3   Monitor, Keyboard, Disk Drive

A computer's ability to compute depends on several internal elements. One of them is a microprocessor or CPU (Central Processing Unit), the famous computer on a chip. A chip is a platform on which the microprocessor is located. Although a computer is full of chips, only the CPU is capable of computing. All the others are only helpers

1-4   Monitor, Printer

for the CPU, storing information that the CPU needs for computing. The function of the CPU is to receive data in the form of numbers, to store them for later processing, to perform arithmetic and logic operations on data, and output through a disk drive, a monitor, or printer. A typical microprocessor is as small as the end of your finger, but is responsible for directing traffic in the computer (Diagram 1-1).

Another factor that determines a computer's ability to compute is its internal memory. Internal memory is an array or a grid of chips inside a computer that holds all the machine's stored information or unused memory sections. One section of memory comes from the factory already filled with important information that can't be changed by you or the computer. This inalterable, long-term part of memory is called Read Only Memory, (ROM), because the CPU can read this data but can't write in any new data. The basic instructions in today's pocket calculators are ROMs.

Another section of internal memory is empty and can be filled with instructions for the particular task the operator wants the computer to perform. All data in this part of the memory are easily altered from the keyboard or disk drive. When you enter instructions into the computer, these instructions are stored in this part of memory. The information held in this erasable, short-term memory section can be altered to your liking, then stored on a diskette for future use, because it would be lost when the power is turned off. This alterable part of memory is designed to make it easy for the CPU to compute. It allows

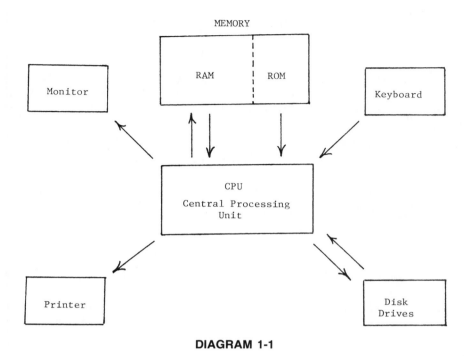

DIAGRAM 1-1

the CPU to take needed data randomly, without having to go through rows of irrelevant data to reach it. Therefore, this part of memory is called Random Access Memory (RAM). The more RAM a computer has, the more it can do. A computer with more RAM can be loaded with longer, more useful instructions.

The size of a computer's memory, ROM and RAM, is measured in a unit called a byte. A byte is simply an eight-place code that stands for a single character (letter, number, or symbol). Each place in the code is called a bit which is a shortened form of binary digit. A bit can only be a one (1) or a zero (0), which are the binary digits, but this is all that a computer needs and can use. The computer uses bytes the same way we use letters and numbers, or the way football coaches use Xs and Os. By stringing bytes into vast arrays or patterns, a computer can count, spell, or draw pictures. A computer stores these bytes by the thousands. Approximately 1,000 bytes, called a kilobyte or K, is the standard measure of memory size in personal computers. For example, 64K RAM means that a computer's random access memory can hold approximately 64,000 bytes of information. The more bytes of information the RAM can hold, the more the computer can do.

THE PERSONAL COMPUTER

When you are in the market for a personal computer, first consider the machine's preferred features that will fulfill your minimum requirements, and then its secondary uses as your application needs increase. Determine what you are getting for the base price and anticipate what it will cost to expand your system. In the long run, the latter is the more important figure.

Before going into specifics, three things to keep in mind are:

1. Maintenance support
2. Feel of the computer
3. Software available

Before you buy any equipment make sure that it can be serviced in a reasonable amount of time by a trained technician. When your computer is down, so is your computerized scouting system. Double-check the servicing aspect. Second, try the equipment out. Take it for a test run as you would a new car. Watching a sales representative's fingers dance across the keys might be fine for an introductory demonstration, but you need to get your own hands on the keyboard. Most computer stores have demonstration hardware and canned exercises which are there for your use. Third, make sure you buy the right hardware for the software you intend to use. We'll discuss software in Chapter 11.

The most important considerations in selecting the right personal computer for your needs concern the following:

1. Keyboard
2. Display
3. Memory
4. Expansion slots
5. Documentation

When trying the keyboard, note the following:

1. Check the size of the keys and the space between them. Where computers are concerned, it used to be that smaller meant better. However, if you're a former defensive tackle with large hands, a small keyboard is of no advantage to you. A standard typewriter size keyboard is best.

2. Check the feel of the keys as you use them. Whether you use the hunt-and-peck method or are an accomplished typist, the touch-type feel of a computer's keys is important.
3. Check to see if a separate numeric pad is available similar to an adding machine or hand-held calculator. Depending on the scouting system you choose, the majority of information you will be entering into the computer may be numeric, and a separate numeric pad may be more convenient than the placement of numbers on a standard typewriter.
4. Check to see that the keyboard is of the ASCII (American Standard Code for Information Interchange) variety. This will insure the inclusion of upper-case and lower-case letters, all numbers to 9, all necessary punctuation marks, and all necessary computer control codes. You should also find out if there are any added functions included.

One final word before we move on to the next consideration. When we were discussing the bit and the byte in the beginning of this section, we stated that a byte is simply an eight-place code that stands for a single character (letter, number, or symbol), that each place in the code is called a bit (binary digit), and that a bit can only be a one (1) or a zero (0). In the ASCII system the letter A is represented by the byte 01000001, and there are 256 different arrangements of bits into bytes that can be used to represent different letters, numbers, symbols, and functions. The ASCII makes life easier for all computer users by standardizing the code used for representing information inside a computer, for transmitting information between a computer and an input-output device, and for transmitting information between computers.

The second consideration is display. The personal computer can only display letters, numbers, and symbols in a prescribed number of rows (lines) and columns (characters). The standard display of most personal computers is 24 rows (lines) of 40 columns (characters). You may want 24 lines of 80 characters. Computers with this capacity are available, but are more expensive. Another display consideration is the possibility of graphics. Graphics are pictures, diagrams, or images either in two tones or color. We will have more to say about display later on when we discuss video monitors.

Your third consideration, which may be the most important one, is the amount of user memory available. Nothing is more frustrating than to enter all the data for the last three games of your arch rival, hit the appropriate keys, and see an OUT OF MEMORY ERROR message displayed on the monitor. This means your computer is overloaded. Always buy the most memory you can possibly afford. With most personal computer systems 32K is a minimum, 48K is nice to have, but 64K is best of all. We're talking about 64K of user available memory in RAM. Make sure that you purchase the necessary adapter boards or cards which will keep the printer, disk drive, language (see Chapter 11), and monitor from using up valuable RAM for their operation. You want all the RAM for the operation of your computerized scouting system and storage of your data.

If you do find that you need more RAM after your initial purchase, ask yourself the following:

1. Do I need to simply add memory chips or do I need to buy a memory board with control circuits to expand RAM?
2. Are the memory chips compatible with my system?
3. Can the chips in my system make use of all the memory that is available?

The fourth important consideration deals with the expansion slots. Expansion slots are the locations into which you can plug the adapter boards or cards for your input-output devices. Make sure they are easily accessible.

Your last consideration in the purchase of your personal computer is documentation. Documentation includes all the written material such as owner's manuals that come with the hardware. Skim the pages and look for the following:

1. Is it written so a beginner can understand it?
2. Are there plenty of pictures and diagrams?
3. Is there a glossary of terms in the back with definitions that can be understood?
4. Does it contain a section on where to go for help if you have a problem?

THE DISK DRIVE

Most early personal computers used cassette tapes and cassette recorders for input and storage, but modern disk drives are superior. A disk drive moves data with far greater efficiency and reliability, and despite its higher cost is really the only practical device for most applications. In other words, spend the extra money that a disk drive will cost and spare yourself the frustration of using a cassette. You need to consider the following when purchasing a disk drive and its DOS (Disk Operating System):

1. Are the controller circuits on the expansion card and connecting cables compatible with my personal computer?
2. What is its storage capacity?
3. How is its reliability?
4. Are the necessary instructions available to make the system work?
5. Does it use RAM?

THE MONITOR

Originally, an ordinary television set with a special adapter called an RF modulator attached was the most common visual output device used with personal computers. Now special video monitors are sold with most personal computers. A video monitor that is made exclusively for use with the computer offers a basic but significant advantage over an ordinary TV set—a monitor is designed to give sharper images. This is more convenient when you are working with a screen full of numbers or words. A video monitor does not function as a TV set when detached from the computer. It only runs on computer signals.

To avoid any problems, simply buy your monitor at the same time you buy your personal computer and disk drive. Quite often these three items will be sold together as a complete system. Have the sales representative display numbers and letters on the screen at both 40 and 80 characters per line. Know how your scouting report will be displayed on the monitor before you buy. It does no good to have a screen full of numbers or letters that you can't read or that cause eye strain.

Black and white monitors are the least expensive. Monitors with green or blue-green screens will help lessen eye fatigue. The latest monitors even have light tan or amber screens. If your computer is capable of color graphics, then you may want a color monitor. Have the sales representative show you a graphics display which includes letters and numbers on a color monitor. You will notice color fringes around the letters and numbers which can cause eye fatigue. Unfortunately we can't have the best of both worlds yet.

The term *pixel* refers to the dots of light that form the image on the monitor of a personal computer. The more pixels that a monitor has the sharper its images will be, and the more you will pay for it. Have the salesman demonstrate monitors with different numbers of pixels. The number of pixels in a horizontal row and a vertical column is an important specification.

THE PRINTER

It is a fact of computing life that printers cannot print data as fast as computers can transmit data. This may not seem critical until you're running hard copy for your next football staff meeting and you realize that the numbers on the monitor are not appearing as fast as they were before you turned on the printer. My advice is to plan ahead and allow yourself more time for your next printout. It is also true that a top of the line printer may cost as much or more than a computer. The reason is that printer technology has not kept pace with computer technology, but that may change in the near future. A printer is a mechanical device and is therefore inherently slower than the electronic device that feeds it—the personal computer.

When you buy a printer for under $1,000, you are playing a game of speed (how fast do you need a copy?) versus print quality (does it look as if a typewriter did it?). If a major breakthrough occurs and someone starts selling a printer with a speed of 100 cps (characters per second) of typewriter quality with a three-digit price tag, buy one immediately, because they won't stay on the shelves very long. Until that occurs, follow these guidelines when you purchase your printer:

1. Buy a printer that is capable of graphics and has as few moving parts as possible. A dot-matrix printer that represents characters with a pattern of dots like the pattern of lights that forms the numbers on an athletic scoreboard is usually your best choice.
2. Buy a printer capable of at least 80 cps, but 160 cps capability is available on some of the new models.
3. Buy a printer with an adjustable tractor-type pin feed.
4. Buy continuous feed paper (fanfold paper), which is one long strip of paper with a horizontal perforated line at the break between each sheet, and edges with holes that can be removed by tearing vertically.
5. Check the cost of replacing ribbons or ribbon cartridges.

6. Check the availability of a trained technician to service the machine.
7. Avoid printer-driver systems that use valuable RAM space. Use an adapter board that plugs into one of the expansion slots.
8. Buy a printer capable of the correct number of characters per line for the scouting system you choose. The more characters per line your system requires (40, 80, or 132), the more your printer will cost.
9. Buy a printer with an easily interchangeable printer head.
10. Check on printer buffers, which are adapter cards that will allow you to use your printer without tying up your personal computer. You may then continue to use your computer as the printer prints hard copy.

THE JOYSTICK

A joystick is the handle used to play video games. If your scouting program is menu-driven then you may need to buy a joystick. A menu is a list of choices presented by the computer on the monitor, from which the user makes his selection. This is in contrast to entering data through the keyboard in numerical form.

THE POWER STRIP

If you run out of convenient electrical outlets where you can plug in your computer, your monitor, and your printer all at the same time, buy a power strip that requires only one wall socket. There are also devices that serve the same function, and act as surge protectors to prevent strange things from happening inside your computer, because the air conditioner came on causing a power surge throughout the electrical system. This may send unwanted signals to your computer.

THE SALES BROCHURES

It's a lot of fun to read most of the sales brochures describing personal computers. The story line is exciting, and the pictures of all that hardware are great. However, once you have made your way past the sales pitch, scrutinize the technical specifications as carefully as possible. You will come across many of the terms we have discussed and some we haven't. If there is something you don't understand, ask the sales representative and make sure that he can explain it in terms you can understand. If not, find another sales person or visit another computer store.

THE COST

We have given you an overview of personal computers—what they are both inside and outside, what parts are included in hardware, and how to shop for just the right combination for your needs.

At today's prices the cost of a computer system suitable for the needs of a high school or athletic department would be in the range of $1,000 to $3,700. This would include the cost of the computer, keyboard, monitor, and disk drive. The addition of a printer will add from $300 to $2,000. Does that appear high? It shouldn't. It is about the same as the cost of buying and processing 16mm game film over a two-year period, and less if you buy your own camera, not to mention the added cost of a good football analyst projector or two. Or, compare it with the amount of money that can be invested in the machines, racks, bars, and weights in a well-equipped weight room. Or, total the amount spent on seven-, five-, two-, and one-man blocking and tackling sleds. All of this equipment is, of course, essential to a competitive football program. We feel that a personal computer is now in the same category.

CHAPTER 2

TRAINING YOUR SCOUTS

Before you can implement a successful computerized scouting system, you must have capable personnel to attend the games and collect the raw data which will be used by your personal computer to analyze your opponents. We are, of course, talking about the scouts. You will find a wide variation in their observational abilities, knowledge of football, and devotion to their task. A well-trained set of scouting teams and a well-organized scouting system are essentials if you hope to tap the full potential of your personal computer in the analysis of your opponents' offensive strategies.

In this chapter we will describe the optimum training routine to insure that your scouts will bring back the best possible information. We start with our Scouting Manual and the use of transparencies and slides as training devices. The viewing of game films and scrimmages in a progressive sequence are also discussed as part of their training. The culmination of this training will be the additional experience gained by the scouts as the season starts and the reporting routine begins.

THE SCOUTING MANUAL

Our scouting manual is collated by the scouting coordinator the first week of August. We use a mimeograph machine to run as many copies of each form as will be needed for the entire football season. After all copies are run, holes are punched in the sheets and they are placed in spiral binders to insure that no pages will be misplaced and mixed with the wrong game or wrong team. Each manual is labeled with the name of the team being scouted and the head scout. All manuals are stored in chronological order in a filing cabinet in the coach's office. No

new manual is ever handed out until the information from the previous game has been turned in. Upon receiving the completed data
from the head scout, the scouting coordinator will remove the binder,
organize the material by section, and file the information in a separate
folder by team. In this way we can build a progressive picture of an
opponent until the final composite is put together the weekend before
the actual game.

The manual is composed of the following sections:

1. Cover Sheet (green)—This includes the name of team to be
   scouted and the head scout.
2. Kicking Game Worksheet—This includes two diagrams of a
   football field from our opponent's 35 yard line to our end line.
   One diagram is for their kickoff coverage and the other diagram is for their kickoff return. On the kickoff coverage diagram, we request that the scouts identify by jersey number
   the scouted team's personnel with their initial spacing. We
   ask for the distance of each kick to be marked with an X and
   the lane assignments of each defender to be indicated with
   arrows. Of special importance are the players who will contain any sideline returns, arrive at the ball first, and act as a
   safety. On the kickoff return diagram, we ask the scouts to
   again identify by jersey number the scouted team's personnel
   in their respective positions. The actual return is diagramed
   with arrows with special attention being given to any desig-
   nated return man, his personal protectors, and those setting
   the wedge on a middle return or the wall on a sideline return
   (Form 2-1).
3. Kicking Game Worksheet—This sheet is divided into thirds
   and is used to diagram our opponent's punt coverage, punt
   return, and extra point. We are most concerned with the actual formations in these three phases of the kicking game. The
   coverage patterns and rush patterns of the first two are drawn
   with arrows. Any comments on trick plays should be included (Form 2-2).
4. Divider (yellow)
5. Summary of Offensive Personnel—This sheet is a position
   diagram of our opponent's base set with each individual player's name, jersey number, grade in school, height, weight,
   and pertinent comments included (Form 2-3).

FORM 2-1   Kicking Game Worksheet

KICKOFF RETURN

KICKOFF COVERAGE

0 5 10 15 20 25 30 35 40 45 50 45 40 35

15

Extra Point

Punt Return

Punt Coverage

FORM 2-3   Offensive Personnel

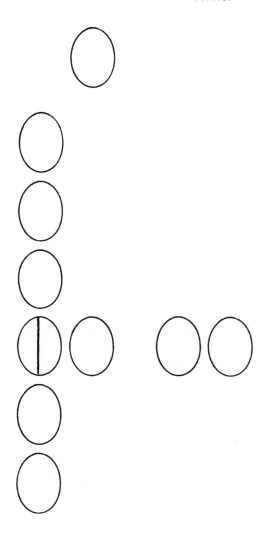

6. Offensive Scouting Form (20 sheets)—This form is the mainstay of our computerized offensive scouting. We will discuss its use in more detail in Chapters 4 and 5 (Form 2-4).

7. Offensive Formations Worksheet (2 sheets)—This sheet is divided into twelve sections for diagraming all sets, motions, and shifts used by our opponent. The number of times each variation is utilized is also recorded (Form 2-5).

8. Divider (orange)

9. Summary of Defensive Personnel—This sheet is a position diagram of our opponent's base defense with each individual player's name, jersey number, grade in school, height, weight, and pertinent comments included (Form 2-6).

10. Defensive Fronts and Coverages Worksheet (2 sheets)—This sheet is divided into six sections for diagraming all fronts, stunts, coverages, blitzes, rushes, drops, and adjustments used by our opponent (Form 2-7).

11. Defensive Situations Worksheet (2 sheets)—This sheet is divided into nine sections for diagraming our opponent's defenses used in short yardage, long yardage, and goal line situations (Form 2-8).

12. Back Sheet (blue)

TRANSPARENCIES AND SLIDES

After all the scouting manuals have been collated, each scout is given his own sample copy and the scouting coordinator discusses each sheet during our preseason football staff meetings. We have found that the use of an overhead projector, transparencies of the forms, and a water-soluble marking pen are effective audio-visual aids in the explanation of the proper use of each form.

Since it is extremely important that our scouts be able to instantly recognize the offensive formations and defensive sets of a given opponent, and be able to use our terminology in their description, we have put together a file of 35mm slides that includes all of the offensive formations and defensive alignments known to be used by our opponents. We have found that in training our scouts in set recognition, the optimum view is from behind the offense or defense. These slides are taken in the spring so that they will be ready for our coaches' preseason meetings. We use our own players as actors, a series of flash cards, and a shooting script to make sure we cover all the variations.

FORM 2-4   Offensive Scouting Form

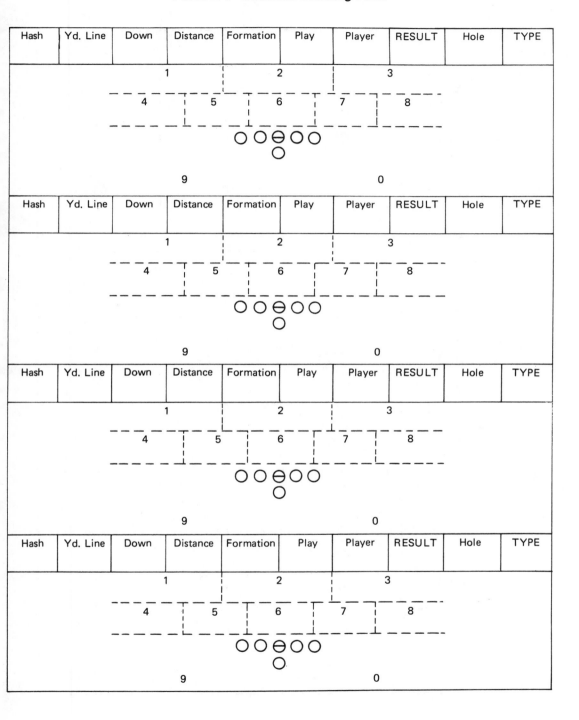

Hash	Yd. Line	Down	Distance	Formation	Play	Player	RESULT	Hole	TYPE

Hash	Yd. Line	Down	Distance	Formation	Play	Player	RESULT	Hole	TYPE

Hash	Yd. Line	Down	Distance	Formation	Play	Player	RESULT	Hole	TYPE

Hash	Yd. Line	Down	Distance	Formation	Play	Player	RESULT	Hole	TYPE

FORM 2-6   Defensive Personnel

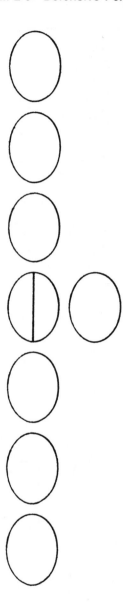

FORM 2-7 Defensive Fronts and Coverages Worksheet

FORM 2-8   Defensive Situations Worksheet

By using a 35mm camera, a 70-210/f/4 zoom lens, and Kodak Ektachrome 200 film, we have produced an excellent set of slides for our purposes. We photograph the offensive formations and defensive alignments from the back from on top of our stadium stands with the sun at the photographer's back. For bright sunshine we use an aperture of f/11 and a shutter speed of 1/250. The photographer must pay special attention to focusing the camera because the longer focal lengths of the zoom lens provide less depth of field (fewer objects in focus). However, since the subject is stationary, you may use a slower shutter speed and a smaller aperture opening to increase the depth of field and focusing becomes less critical. With the slower shutter speed you may want to use a tripod to steady the camera, and a cable release.

Once our slides have been processed, we store them in two Carousel slide holders—one for the offensive formations and one for the defensive alignments. The scouts are given a key with all the formations and sets labeled using our terminology. For some examples see Diagrams 2-1 through 2-6. We have found that flashing these slides on the screen is an excellent training aid for our scouts. The slides also serve as a quick reference just before a scout leaves to watch a game.

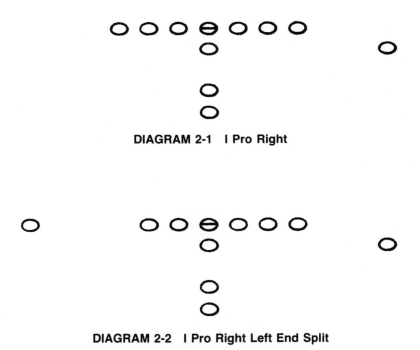

DIAGRAM 2-1   I Pro Right

DIAGRAM 2-2   I Pro Right Left End Split

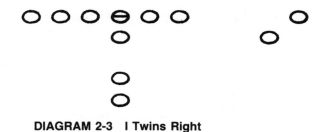

DIAGRAM 2-3   I Twins Right

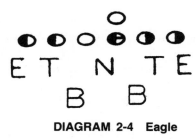

DIAGRAM 2-4   Eagle

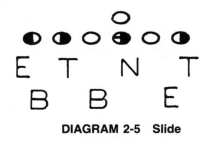

DIAGRAM 2-5   Slide

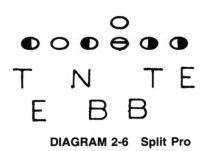

DIAGRAM 2-6   Split Pro

SPRING GAMES AND SCRIMMAGES

In Texas, at the 5A high school level, we have the advantage of three weeks of spring practice culminated by an intra-squad scrimmage. We will send scouting teams to our opponents' spring games in order to help them sharpen their skills. In the summer we are allowed three weeks of practice before our first regularly scheduled game the first weekend in September. During the second week of summer practice we are allowed to have a scrimmage with another high school team in our area. These scrimmages are highly controlled with the ball being placed on a given yard line and the offense allowed a given number of plays to score. Down and distance situations are honored, but usually no phase of the kicking game is practiced. Our opponents are also having their own scrimmages with other schools and our scouts cover these too. This gives them another opportunity to sharpen their skills.

GAME FILMS

Our film cabinet contains 16mm game films of our opponents over the last three years and our scouts have continuous access to a projector and these films. We encourage them to scout a given opponent off a previous year's film. This, of course, has the advantage of allowing the scouts to rerun given plays as they chart the action. During the season we will exchange two films with our opponents. The scouts have access to these also. We will say more about film exchange in the next chapter.

GAMES

Each scouting team will scout an opponent at least three times once the season is underway. The scouting ability of our personnel will continue to improve as the season progresses, after a firm indoctrination has been established through the use of the scouting manual, transparencies, slides, spring games, scrimmages, and game films. Our final goal is to have a set of scouts who know the game, know what to watch for and how to note it down, and are very conscientious. Well-trained scouts are the backbone of our computerized approach to football.

CHAPTER **3**

ORGANIZING YOUR SYSTEM

Even with a group of highly trained scouts at your disposal, you need a system to make sure that the right people get to the right place at the right time with the right instructions once the season is underway. This system must be set up during the summer. For us it entails making up a master scout schedule, a master film exchange schedule, a scouting teams schedule, and a set of general guidelines for effective scouting procedures. With this accomplished, the computerized scouting system will run smoothly throughout the season.

MASTER SCOUT SCHEDULE

The master scout schedule is the keystone of our computerized scouting system. On one chart we itemize our complete schedule and the complete schedule of all of our opponents including day of the week, date, stadium, and whether the game is home or away. We also have developed a simple coding system to keep track of the following:

1. Which scout team is responsible for a given opponent—numbers 1 through 6.
2. Whether the varsity staff will be available to scout—a V.
3. Whether a film exchange needs to be or has been made—an F or Fx.
4. Whether a scouting manual has been issued—an M.
5. Whether a given game was won or lost by a past or future opponent—a W or L.
6. If the scouting report has been turned in and filed—an open ○.

7. If the scouting report has been coded for computer input—a closed ●.
8. If the coded report has been entered into the computer and stored on a diskette—an X.
9. Whether the scouting report has been checked by film—a C.
10. The win-loss record of each opponent both overall and in district or conference play is given at the end of each row.

The schedule is compiled in the summer as our opponents send us their master schedules, and is checked through various sports news media such as newspapers and magazines. A typical master scout schedule is shown (Schedule 3-2) and specific notations are marked (Schedule 3-1), and discussed.

In Schedule 3-1, we are scheduled to play Katy, there (T), on October 15. We scouted their game against Eisenhower on October 1. Scout team number two (2) was assigned this game. We have exchanged game films (Fx). The scouting manual was issued (M). Katy played Eisenhower at home (H). Katy lost the game (L). The coded report has been entered into the computer and stored on a diskette (X). The scouting report has been checked by film (C).

SCHEDULE 3-1

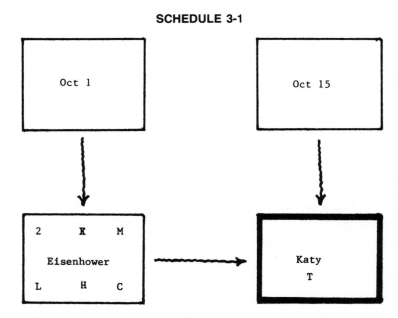

SCHEDULE 3-2 Master Scout Schedule

Master Scout Schedule

Sep 3	Sep 10	Sep 17	Sep 24	Oct 1	Oct 8	Oct 15	Oct 22	Oct 29	Nov 5
Kingwood	Huntsville	Nimitz	New Caney	Westfield	Humble	Conroe	Spring	Temple	McCullough
Conroe	Aldine	McCullough	J.Village	Cy-Creek	Nimitz	Eisenhower	F.Brook	Smiley	Mac-Arthur
Eisenhower	Cy-Fair	Westfield	Spring	Kingwood	McCullough	New Caney	S.Jesuit	Humble	Conroe
McCullough	Klein	Conroe	Mac-Arthur	Cy-Fair	Smiley	F.Brook	Nimitz	Eisenhower	Aldine
Sharpstown	Lee	Bellaire	Cy-Creek	Waltrip	Reagan	Washington	Scarbrough	Kashmere	South Houston
Lamar	Spring	Alief Hastings	Aldine	Scarbrough	J.Village	Cy-Fair	Cy-Creek	Klein	Katy
Katy Taylor	Stratford	Alief Elsik	Nimitz	Eisenhower	Cy-Creek	Katy	Klein	Cy-Fair	J.Village
Westbury	Westfield	West-chester	McCullough	Mac-Arthur	Klein	J.Village	Cy-Fair	Katy	Cy-Creek
Northbrook	Nimitz	S.Branch	Waltrip	Aldine	Katy	Klein	J.Village	Cy-Creek	Cy-Fair
Humble	Mac-Arthur	Washington	Eisenhower	Nimitz	Cy-Fair	Cy-Creek	Katy	J.Village	Klein

MASTER FILM EXCHANGE SCHEDULE

We store all of our game films for the last three years in a cabinet in the head coach's office. Each 16mm canister has its own slot. There are 20 slots per row and four rows total. (Photo 3-1). This allows us to store regular season game films for a given year in a single row. All scrimmages and spring game films for the last two years are kept in the bottom row. The cabinet is kept locked for security. The scouting coordinator working with the head coach is responsible for film exchange.

Notations on a chart inside the cabinet enable us to know where our films have been, where they are now, and where they will be in the future. Our opponents are listed at the beginning of the rows down the left margin in chronological order, and the seven-day time frames for film exchange from the beginning of the season to the end

3-1 Film storage

of the season are listed at the top of the columns. In the spaces at the intersection between the rows and columns, we pencil in the name of the school that has had the film, has it at present, or has been promised access to it. Also included in the cabinet is a complete listing of school, head coach, film exchange coordinator, and athletic department phone numbers for both school hours and night-weekend numbers for quick reference. Included is an example of our master film exchange chart (Schedule 3-3).

SCOUTING TEAMS SCHEDULE

Each scout is given a schedule of his game assignments at the beginning of the year. The information is taken from the master scout schedule but is presented in a different form for easy interpretation by the scouting groups. We use our computer and an information management system developed for it. We may then have the computer print out the schedule by groups (Printout 3-1), by dates (Printout 3-2), or in any other format we choose. We also use this system to print the labels for our scouting manuals (Printout 3-3).

GUIDELINES FOR EFFECTIVE SCOUTING

We have found that the following additional guidelines assure effective scouting procedures:

1. The first coach listed in each group is the head scout and is responsible for turning in all reports, forms, expenses, etc. to the scouting coordinator.
2. The head scout should coordinate with the scouting coordinator on the exchange of game films the week that a district opponent is scouted *for the final time.*
3. Each group will be present at our games when we play the team that group scouted. Their presence in the press box is essential.
4. The coded report *for each game* is due in the field house by *8 a.m. the day after each game* is scouted. This will allow the game to be put into the computer as soon as possible.
5. Any questions on scouting procedures should be directed to the scouting coordinator.

SCHEDULE 3-3 Master Film Exchange Schedule

File: Varsity Scouting
Report: Scouting Groups
Page 1
Jul 21, 1983

Group	Coaches	Team	Date		Opponent	Stadium	Time	Comment
01	Pell,Rabender	Aldine	SEP	3	Conroe	Thorne	7:30	Film Ex
01	Pell,Rabender	Jersey Village	SEP	17	Alief Hastings	A.I.S.D.	7:30	
01	Pell,Rabender	Jersey Village	SEP	25	Aldine	CF.I.S.D.	7:30	Sat
01	Pell,Rabender	Jersey Village	OCT	1	Scarborough	Delmar	7:30	Film Ex
02	King,Huckaby	Westfield	SEP	2	Eisenhower	Thorne	7:30	Thu
02	King,Huckaby	Westfield	SEP	10	Cy-Fair	S.I.S.D.	7:30	Film Ex
02	King,Huckaby	Katy	SEP	24	Nimitz	Thorne	7:30	
02	King,Huckaby	Katy	OCT	1	Eisenhower	Ka.I.S.D.	7:30	
02	King,Huckaby	Katy	OCT	8	Cy-Creek	CF.I.S.D.	7:30	Film Ex
03	Ray,Bartlett	MacArthur	SEP	3	McCullough	C.I.S.D.	7:30	
03	Ray,Bartlett	MacArthur	SEP	10	Klein	Thorne	7:30	
03	Ray,Bartlett	MacArthur	SEP	17	Conroe	C.I.S.D.	7:30	Film Ex
03	Ray,Bartlett	Cy-Fair	OCT	1	MacArthur	CF.I.S.D.	7:30	
03	Ray,Bartlett	Cy-Fair	OCT	9	Klein	CF.I.S.D.	7:30	Sat
03	Ray,Bartlett	Cy-Fair	OCT	15	Jersey Village	CF.I.S.D.	7:30	Film Ex
04	Frazier,Maly	Waltrip	SEP	10	Lee	Delmar	7:30	
04	Frazier,Maly	Waltrip	SEP	16	Bellaire	Delmar	7:30	Thu
04	Frazier,Maly	Waltrip	SEP	25	Cy-Creek	Delmar	7:30	Sat/FEx
05	Sands,Hennig	Cy-Creek	OCT	8	Katy	CF.I.S.D.	7:30	
05	Sands,Hennig	Cy-Creek	OCT	15	Klein	K.I.S.D.	7:30	
05	Sands,Hennig	Cy-Creek	OCT	23	Jersey Village	CF.I.S.D.	7:30	Sat/FEx
06	Rice,Thornton	Klein	OCT	15	Cy-Creek	K.I.S.D.	7:30	
06	Rice,Thornton	Klein	OCT	22	Katy	K.I.S.D.	7:30	
06	Rice,Thornton	Klein	OCT	29	Jersey Village	CF.I.S.D.	7:30	Film Ex
07	Varsity Staff	Westfield	SEP	2	Eisenhower	Thorne	7:30	Thu
07	Varsity Staff	Waltrip	SEP	16	Bellaire	Delmar	7:30	Thu
07	Varsity Staff	Katy	SEP	24	Nimitz	Thorne	7:30	
07	Varsity Staff	Jersey Village	SEP	25	Aldine	CF.I.S.D.	7:30	Sat
07	Varsity Staff	Klein/Cy-Fair	OCT	9	Cy-Fair/Klein	CF.I.S.D.	7:30	Sat
07	Varsity Staff	Cy-Creek	OCT	23	Jersey Village	CF.I.S.D.	7:30	Sat

PRINTOUT 3-2

```
File:    Varsity Scouting
Report:  Scouting Sequence                                              Page 1
                                                                        Jul 21, 1983
Date   Group Coaches         Team              Opponent         Stadium    Time  Comment
-----  ----- -------------   ---------------   --------------   --------   ----  --------
SEP 2  02    King,Huckaby    Westfield         Eisenhower       Thorne     7:30  Thu
SEP 2  07    Varsity Staff   Westfield         Eisenhower       Thorne     7:30  Thu
SEP 3  01    Pell,Rabender   Aldine            Conroe           Thorne     7:30  Film Ex
SEP 3  03    Ray,Bartlett    MacArthur         McCullough       C.I.S.D.   7:30
SEP 10 02    King,Huckaby    Westfield         Cy-Fair          S.I.S.D.   7:30  Film Ex
SEP 10 03    Ray,Bartlett    MacArthur         Klein            Thorne     7:30
SEP 10 04    Frazier,Maly    Waltrip           Lee              Delmar     7:30
SEP 16 04    Frazier,Maly    Waltrip           Bellaire         Delmar     7:30  Thu
SEP 16 07    Varsity Staff   Waltrip           Bellaire         Delmar     7:30  Thu
SEP 17 01    Pell,Rabender   Jersey Village    Alief Hastings   A.I.S.D.   7:30
SEP 17 03    Ray,Bartlett    MacArthur         Conroe           C.I.S.D.   7:30  Film Ex
SEP 24 02    King,Huckaby    Katy              Nimitz           Thorne     7:30
SEP 24 07    Varsity Staff   Katy              Nimitz           Thorne     7:30
SEP 25 01    Pell,Rabender   Jersey Village    Aldine           CF.I.S.D.  7:30  Bat
SEP 25 04    Frazier,Maly    Waltrip           Cy-Creek         Delmar     7:30  Sat/FEx
SEP 25 07    Varsity Staff   Jersey Village    Aldine           CF.I.S.D.  7:30  Sat
OCT 1  01    Pell,Rabender   Jersey Village    Scarborough      Delmar     7:30  Film Ex
OCT 1  02    King,Huckaby    Katy              Eisenhower       Ka.I.S.D.  7:30
OCT 1  03    Ray,Bartlett    Cy-Fair           MacArthur        CF.I.S.D.  7:30
OCT 8  02    King,Huckaby    Katy              Cy-Creek         CF.I.S.D.  7:30  Film Ex
OCT 8  05    Sands,Hennig    Cy-Creek          Katy             CF.I.S.D.  7:30
OCT 9  03    Ray,Bartlett    Cy-Fair           Klein            CF.I.S.D.  7:30  Sat
OCT 9  07    Varsity Staff   Klein/Cy-Fair     Cy-Fair/Klein    CF.I.S.D.  7:30  Sat
OCT 15 03    Ray,Bartlett    Cy-Fair           Jersey Village   CF.I.S.D.  7:30  Film Ex
OCT 15 05    Sands,Hennig    Cy-Creek          Klein            K.I.S.D.   7:30
OCT 15 06    Rice,Thornton   Klein             Cy-Creek         K.I.S.D.   7:30
OCT 22 06    Rice,Thornton   Klein             Katy             K.I.S.D.   7:30
OCT 23 05    Sands,Hennig    Cy-Creek          Jersey Village   CF.I.S.D.  7:30  Sat/FEx
OCT 23 07    Varsity Staff   Cy-Creek          Jersey Village   CF.I.S.D.  7:30  Sat
OCT 29 06    Rice,Thornton   Klein             Jersey Village   CF.I.S.D.  7:30  Film Ex
```

King,Huckaby Westfield SEP 2	Frazier,Maly Waltrip SEP 16	Frazier,Maly Waltrip SEP 25
Varsity Staff Westfield SEP 2	Varsity Staff Waltrip SEP 16	Varsity Staff Jersey Village SEP 25
Pell,Rabender Aldine SEP 3	Pell,Rabender Jersey Village SEP 17	Pell,Rabender Jersey Village OCT 1
Ray,Bartlett MacArthur SEP 3	Ray,Bartlett MacArthur SEP 17	King,Huckaby Katy OCT 1
King,Huckaby Westfield SEP 10	King,Huckaby Katy SEP 24	Ray,Bartlett Cy-Fair OCT 1
Ray,Bartlett MacArthur SEP 10	Varsity Staff Katy SEP 24	King,Huckaby Katy OCT 8

6. Any individual traveling on a scouting trip will be reimbursed for mileage and cost of meals. Cash receipts will be required. Such reimbursement for travel should be requested on the regular travel form secured from the athletic office (Form 3-1).

FORM 3-1

ATHLETIC MILEAGE AND MEAL REPORT					
NAME _____		Head Coach's Approval _____			
		Athletic Director _____			
DATE	TO	FOR	MILES	MEALS	TOTAL

7. All available preview material should be studied before a scouting assignment. Such material may include slides, spring games, scrimmages, and past games.

8. The scout team should be organized according to the spotter-recorder system before arriving at the game (see Chapter 4).

9. Scouts should arrive 45 minutes early for game-site scouting, so that they can record preliminary data while the teams warm up.

10. A scout should obtain three programs at the game, so that he can identify offensive starters, defensive starters, and two-way players. We will use pictures and rosters for our motivational posters.

11. Scouts are encouraged to collect newspaper articles on the teams they have scouted. *The Houston Chronicle, Houston Post,* and *Woodland Sun* are good sources. These articles will also be used for our motivational posters.

12. If an emergency situation arises where an individual scout is unable to attend a specific game, he is to contact the scouting coordinator immediately so that a substitute may be assigned.

As the season progresses, unexpected problems will naturally arise, but by organizing your computerized scouting system along the lines we have discussed, you will have the time to attack these problems head on as the rest of your system operates smoothly.

CHAPTER 4

COLLECTING THE DATA

OFFENSIVE SCOUTING FORM

We have discussed training our scouts and organizing our computerized scouting system. It is now time to cover the actual collection of the raw data at the game site or from film breakdown. We are going to establish what is called a data base. This refers to the collection of information which is organized in a form that can be processed by our personal computer. The use of the offensive scouting form accomplishes this and is the crux of our computerized offensive football scouting. Its inclusion in our scouting manual was mentioned in Chapter 2. Note that it is possible to chart four offensive plays on one sheet.

The Offensive Scouting Form (Form 4-1) we use reports ten numerically coded items on each play:

1. Hash (hashmark position of the ball)
2. Yd. line (distance to go for a touchdown)
3. Down
4. Distance (distance to go for a first down)
5. Formation
6. Play
7. Player (jersey number of the ball carrier or intended receiver)
8. Result (net gain or loss)
9. Hole (through which the back ran or zone into which ball was thrown)
10. Type (run, pass, or punt)

FORM 4-1   Offensive Scouting Form

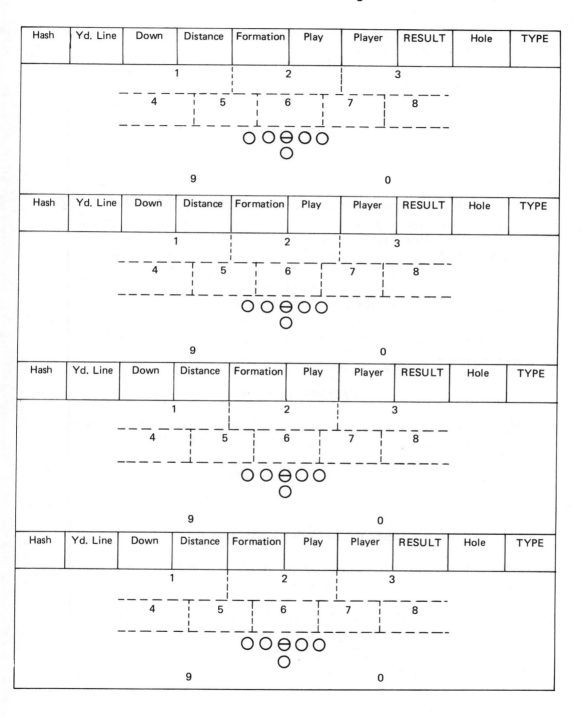

The tendencies and statistics of our opponents are based on these ten pieces of information.

The data recorded on this form are written in the appropriate blocks at four different times:

1. Before the snap
2. During the play
3. After the whistle
4. After the game

At the game site different information is recorded before the snap, during the play, and after the whistle. The recording of data during these three periods will be discussed in this chapter, and a sample charting will be given of four plays in sequence during one offensive possession. In Chapter 5 we will discuss the fourth time period, after the game, when the final blocks are filled in . The raw data are then fed into the computer for final analysis. We will also use our sample possession in Chapter 5 and will follow these four plays through Chapter 8 as we compile, store, display, and break down our information.

BEFORE THE SNAP

The first four pieces of information on the offensive scouting form are recorded while the offensive team is in the huddle. These include:

1. Hash (hashmark position of the ball)
2. Yd. line (distance to go for a touchdown)
3. Down
4. Distance (distance to go for a first down)

The data for each play *must* be in numerical form, therefore we have adopted the following coding system:

1. Hash: This is recorded from the offense's point of view.

   1 = left hash
   2 = middle of the field
   3 = right hash

It is the choice of the defensive coordinator as to whether a 1 or 3 will be recorded only when the ball is directly on the hash or a given number of yards inside the hash.

2. Yd. line: This is recorded as the total distance to go for a touchdown. For example, the offense has the ball on their own 20 yard line. This is recorded as the 80 yard line.

3. Down: This is recorded as any number 1 through 4.

4. Distance: This is recorded as any number of yards (1 through 99) to go for a first down.

As an example, we have coded the first four blocks of information on an offensive scouting form for four plays in sequence during one offensive possession (Form 4-2).

DURING THE PLAY

We use a spotter-recorder system in which one offensive scout is primarily responsible for gathering the data visually and reporting it verbally (the spotter), and the other offensive scout is primarily responsible for writing down the data on the offensive scouting form (the recorder). Of course, once the recorder has written down the before-snap data, he becomes a second set of eyes to watch and then record the following (Diagrams 4-1 through 4-9):

We have found that a lot more information will be brought back if no actual writing is done during the first phases of the play. We also allow our scouts to divide their attention between the nine listed items as talents dictate. However, all of this information is recorded as a diagram on the offensive scouting form as soon as possible.

We have now added this information to the sample form for our four plays (Form 4-3).

FORM 4-2

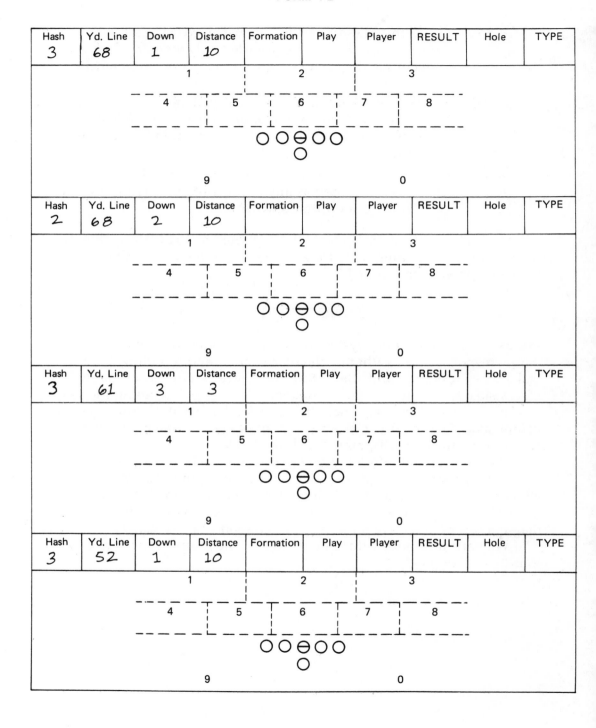

Hash	Yd. Line	Down	Distance	Formation	Play	Player	RESULT	Hole	TYPE
3	68	1	10						

Hash	Yd. Line	Down	Distance	Formation	Play	Player	RESULT	Hole	TYPE
2	68	2	10						

Hash	Yd. Line	Down	Distance	Formation	Play	Player	RESULT	Hole	TYPE
3	61	3	3						

Hash	Yd. Line	Down	Distance	Formation	Play	Player	RESULT	Hole	TYPE
3	52	1	10						

42

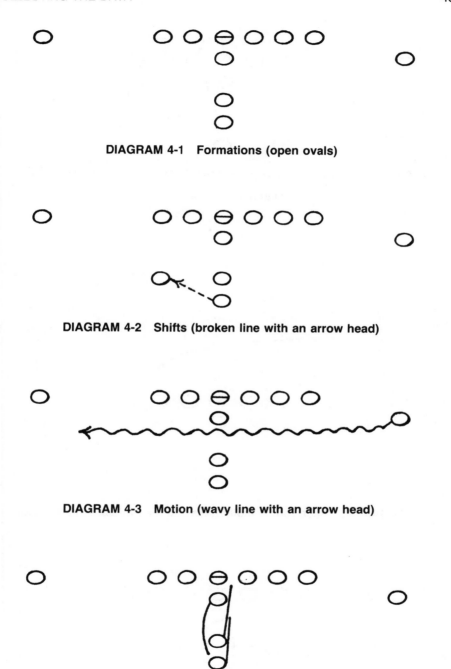

DIAGRAM 4-1 Formations (open ovals)

DIAGRAM 4-2 Shifts (broken line with an arrow head)

DIAGRAM 4-3 Motion (wavy line with an arrow head)

DIAGRAM 4-4 Backfield action (solid lines directed to the point of attack)

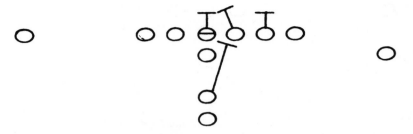

DIAGRAM 4-5   Blocking schemes (solid lines with short perpendicular

segments on the end)

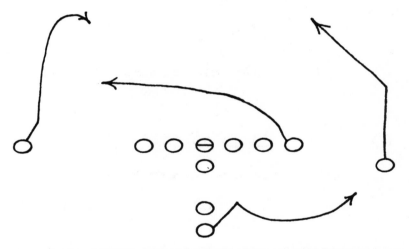

DIAGRAM 4-6   Pass routes (solid lines with arrow heads on the end)

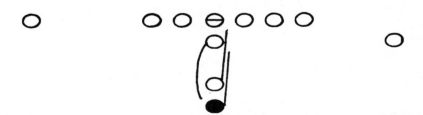

DIAGRAM 4-7   Ball carriers (solid ovals or half solid ovals for options)

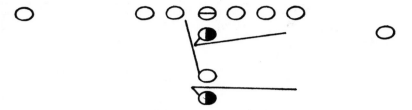

DIAGRAM 4-8   Option

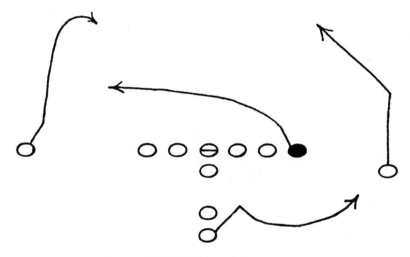

DIAGRAM 4-9   Pass receivers (solid ovals)

FORM 4-3

Hash	Yd. Line	Down	Distance	Formation	Play	Player	RESULT	Hole	TYPE
3	68	1	10						

Hash	Yd. Line	Down	Distance	Formation	Play	Player	RESULT	Hole	TYPE
2	68	2	10						

Hash	Yd. Line	Down	Distance	Formation	Play	Player	RESULT	Hole	TYPE
3	61	3	3						

Hash	Yd. Line	Down	Distance	Formation	Play	Player	RESULT	Hole	TYPE
3	52	1	10						

46

AFTER THE WHISTLE

The last two pieces of information to be recorded during the game include:

1. Player
2. Result

They are recorded as follows:

1. Player: The *jersey number* of the ball carrier or the intended receiver is recorded.
2. Result: The net gain or loss is recorded. If it is a loss, there should be an accompanying negative sign (−).

Form 4-4 has this information added for our four plays.

In order to further explain the above entries and to help the scouting coordinator follow the flow of the game once the completed report has been turned in, we have found the addition of the following information helpful as time permits:

1. Possession number
2. Reason for possession
3. Play number
4. Current score
5. Quarter
6. Time remaining
7. E.O.P. (end of possession)
8. Reason for E.O.P. (punt, fumble lost, pass interception, out of downs, or time expired)
9. Penalties (type and yardage awarded or penalized)
10. Time out

These pieces of information may be recorded to either side of the play diagram.

We have recorded this additional information on Form 4-5. This completes the game phase of our offenive scouting form.

In summary, here is an example of the progressive charting of the first play during the third possession. Of course, information for a

FORM 4-4

Hash	Yd. Line	Down	Distance	Formation	Play	Player	RESULT	Hole	TYPE
3	68	1	10			46	0		

Hash	Yd. Line	Down	Distance	Formation	Play	Player	RESULT	Hole	TYPE
2	68	2	10			46	7		

Hash	Yd. Line	Down	Distance	Formation	Play	Player	RESULT	Hole	TYPE
3	61	3	3			41	9		

Hash	Yd. Line	Down	Distance	Formation	Play	Player	RESULT	Hole	TYPE
3	52	1	10			41	2		

48

FORM 4-5

Hash	Yd. Line	Down	Distance	Formation	Play	Player	RESULT	Hole	TYPE
3	68	1	10			46	0		

3rd possession
punt
16.
3-0
1st quarter
1:35

Hash	Yd. Line	Down	Distance	Formation	Play	Player	RESULT	Hole	TYPE
2	68	2	10			46	7		

17.

Hash	Yd. Line	Down	Distance	Formation	Play	Player	RESULT	Hole	TYPE
3	61	3	3			41			

18.

Hash	Yd. Line	Down	Distance	Formation	Play	Player	RESULT	Hole	TYPE
3	52	1	10			41	2		

19.
2nd quarter

given play would be charted on only one section of the form, but we have divided the play into four steps for emphasis on Form 4-6.

We have discussed the charting of offensive plays for hash, yard line, down, distance, player, and result. We have also shown how to diagram the play and how to add additional comments. During the ball game, hash, yd. line, down, and distance should be recorded before the play starts. The formation and action should be drawn on the scouting form. Player and the result should be recorded after the play is finished.

These procedures may also be followed during film breakdown with the added convenience of instant replays at a push of a button. In Chapter 5 we will discuss how formation, play, hole, and type may be recorded at halftime or after the game.

FORM 4-6

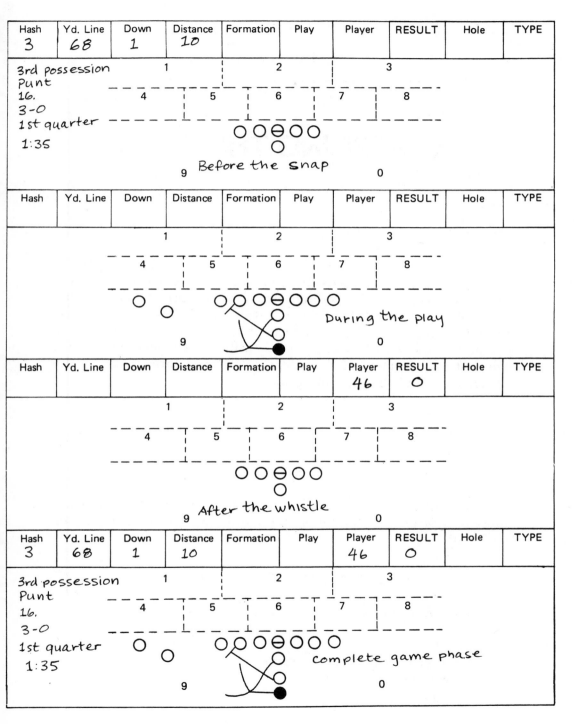

Hash	Yd. Line	Down	Distance	Formation	Play	Player	RESULT	Hole	TYPE
3	68	1	10						

3rd possession
Punt
16.
3-0
1st quarter
1:35

1   2   3
4   5   6   7   8

Before the snap
9   0

Hash	Yd. Line	Down	Distance	Formation	Play	Player	RESULT	Hole	TYPE

1   2   3
4   5   6   7   8

During the play
9   0

Hash	Yd. Line	Down	Distance	Formation	Play	Player	RESULT	Hole	TYPE
						46	O		

1   2   3
4   5   6   7   8

After the whistle
9   0

Hash	Yd. Line	Down	Distance	Formation	Play	Player	RESULT	Hole	TYPE
3	68	1	10			46	O		

3rd possession
Punt
16.
3-0
1st quarter
1:35

1   2   3
4   5   6   7   8

complete game phase
9   0

51

CHAPTER **5**

COMPILING THE DATA

In this chapter we will discuss the completion of the offensive scouting form after the game. The coding system that we use will be included. The system used needs to be flexible. It should always be one in which the information is coded in a form that the computer can process (numeric). It should be compact and easily recognizable by the user. The last four sections of the offensive scouting form (Diagram 4-6) which are completed after the game are:

1. Formation
2. Play
3. Hole
4. Type

All four come from the play diagram as drawn. We will discuss these four pieces of information in the order of type, hole, formation, and play.

FORMATION, HOLE, AND TYPE

Under TYPE, a run, pass, or punt is recorded as follows:

1 = run or scramble
2 = incomplete pass or interception
3 = complete pass or interference
4 = punt or quick kick

Under HOLE, the hole through which the back ran is recorded as follows (Diagram 5-1):

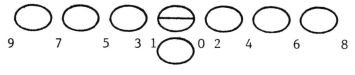

DIAGRAM 5-1

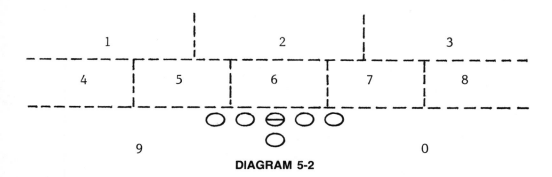

DIAGRAM 5-2

On a pass the zone into which the ball was thrown is recorded. The short zones (numbers 4 through 8) are 15 yards deep. Note that passes behind the line of scrimmage can be recorded as being thrown into the 0 or 9 zone (Diagram 5-2).

Under FORMATION, all formations should be numbered beginning with 1 for the base set and continuing in sequence to the least used formations of a given opponent.

1 = I Pro Right Left End Split	7 = Power I Right
2 = I Pro Left Right End Split	8 = Power I Left
3 = I Twins Right	9 = Spread Right
4 = I Twins Left	10 = Spread Left
5 = I Wing Right Left End Split	11 = Wing Right
6 = I Wing Left Right End Split	12 = Wing Left

This is where the offensive formations worksheet as described in Chapter 2 under the scouting manual can be a big help. If the scouts have completed the worksheet as described, it will be easy for the scouting coordinator and head scout to draw up a formation key as follows (Diagrams 5-3 through 5-8):

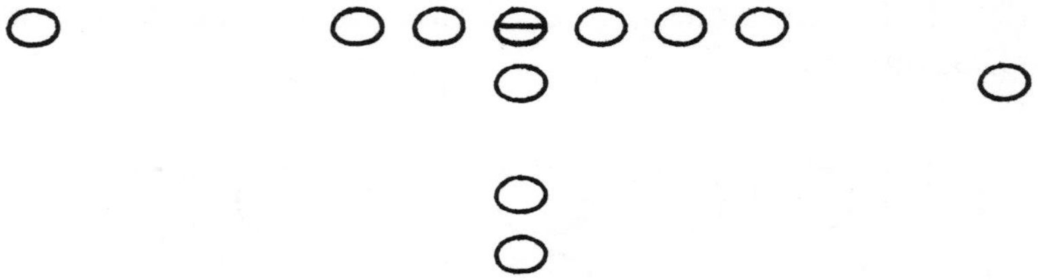

DIAGRAM 5-3   I Pro Right Left End Split

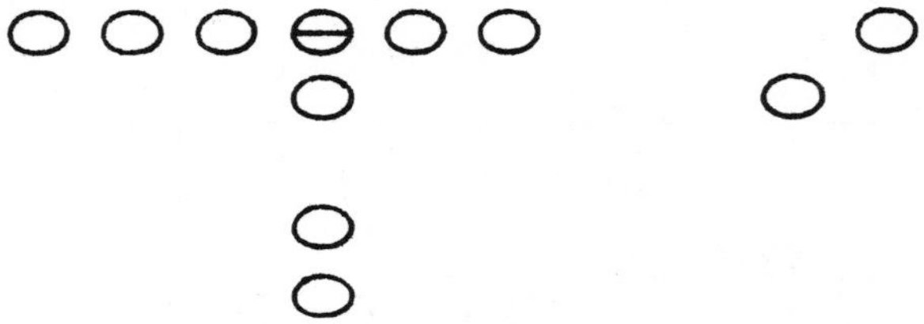

DIAGRAM 5-4   I Twins Right

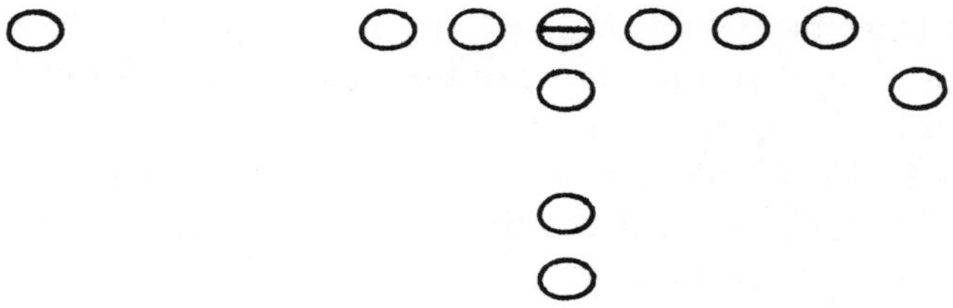

DIAGRAM 5-5   I Wing Right Left End Split

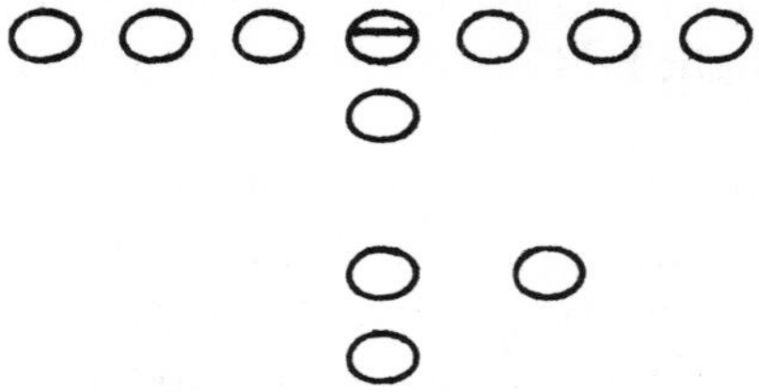

DIAGRAM 5-6   Power I Right

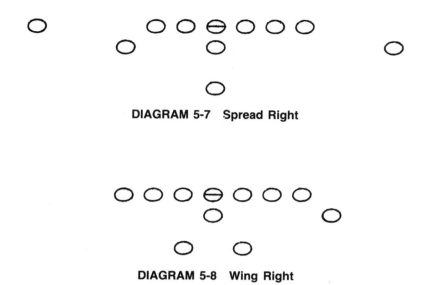

DIAGRAM 5-7 Spread Right

DIAGRAM 5-8 Wing Right

It is the responsibility of the head scout to meet with the scouting coordinator after having seen a team play the first time in order to draw up a tentative formations key. We have found it helpful to train our scouts in set recognition using the slide presentation and terminology sheets described in Chapter 2. Adding the formation, hole, and type information to each one of our four plays from Chapter 4, the offensive scouting form would now look like Form 5-1.

CODING THE PLAY

We have saved the section labeled PLAY for last because it is the most flexible of all the pieces of information that will be recorded on the offensive scouting form. It can be used as simply or as diversely as dictated by the information you wish to extract from your computerized scouting data. Over the years we have become more diverse in the type of information we record under PLAY. Our system dictates that generally under PLAY any two-, three-, or four-digit number is recorded. For running plays the first digit represents the back's position number, the second digit represents the hole through which he ran, the third and fourth digits represent the blocking scheme, the backfield action, or the final ball carrier on an option. For passing plays the first three digits represent the backfield action, and the fourth digit

FORM 5-1

Hash	Yd. Line	Down	Distance	Formation	Play	Player	RESULT	Hole	TYPE
3	68	1	10	4		46	0	7	1

3rd possession
punt
16.
3-0
1st quarter
1:35

Hash	Yd. Line	Down	Distance	Formation	Play	Player	RESULT	Hole	TYPE
2	68	2	10	5		46	7	9	1

17.

Hash	Yd. Line	Down	Distance	Formation	Play	Player	RESULT	Hole	TYPE
3	61	3	3	2		41	9	0	3

18.

Hash	Yd. Line	Down	Distance	Formation	Play	Player	RESULT	Hole	TYPE
3	52	1	10	2		41	2	0	1

19.
2nd quarter

56

represents the route of the primary receiver. Decimal places may be used.

   To remain as flexible as possible in order to scout and analyze the various offenses that we will see during the season, we have developed a standardized coding system. The numbers are arbitrary and can be changed at any time to fit any new system and any different terminology. We present the following coding system only as an example of what we use. It is a system that works for us.

CODING THE RUNNING PLAYS

For running plays the first digit represents the back's position number. We use the following position numbers for split, I, and fullhouse backfields (Diagrams 5-9 through 5-11):

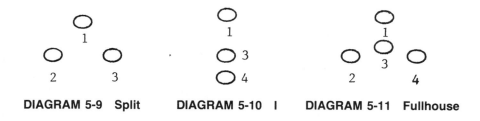

DIAGRAM 5-9   Split   **DIAGRAM 5-10   I**   **DIAGRAM 5-11   Fullhouse**

   The second digit represents the hole through which the back ran (Diagram 5-1). The third and fourth digits represent the blocking scheme, the backfield action, or the final ball carrier on an option. Refer to Table 5-1 for examples. We will not draw the schemes represented in this table, because our terminology may not be the same as your terminology. It does demonstrate, however, the flexibility and compactness of the system.

   Now that we have given an overview of coding the running plays, let's look at our three running plays from Chapter 4—a sprint draw, a toss sweep, and a fullback trap. These plays would be coded as 471.8, 49, and 30.5 respectively. These are interpreted as follows:

Sprint Draw		*Toss Sweep*		*Fullback Trap*	
4	Tailback in the I	4	Tailback in the I	3	Fullback in the I
7	Off tackle left	9	Around left end	0	Right of center
1.8	Sprint draw action			.5	Guard trap

TABLE 5-1

	1 dive	.1 crack	1.1 T-base
option	2 quarterback	.2 combo	1.2 double
	3 pitch	.3 split flow	1.3 hook
	4 G,F,P block	.4 influence trap	1.4 fold
	5 FB opposite	.5 G trap	1.5 veer
bone	6 FB same	.6 T trap	1.6 switch
	7 trick	.7 G,T pull	1.7 loop
	8 lead	.8 waggle	1.8 sprint draw
	9 load	.9 bootleg	1.9 draw
	0 base		
	2.1 log	3.1 down	
	2.2 zone		
	2.3 doodad		
	2.4 scoop		
	2.5 bumpwall		
	2.6 I've got him		
	2.7 E trap		
	2.8 wing fold		
	2.9 cross		

CODING THE PASSING PLAYS

For passing plays the first three digits represent the backfield action and the fourth digit represents the route of the primary receiver. Decimal places may be used for routes. Three examples are as follows:

Play Action	Sprint Out	Drop Back
3 4 2 6	47 1 2	554 0
3 4 3 6	47 2 2	555 0

We like to distinguish between play action, sprint out, and drop back passes. In our scheme these passes would be interpreted as follows:

Play Action

3—Play action

4—I back fake   Isolation fake

2—Ran inside right guard

6—Tight end across

3—Play action

4—I back fake   Isolation fake

3—Ran inside left guard

6—Tight end across

Sprint Out

4—Sprint out
7—Full flow
1—Left side
2—Split end post

4—Sprint out
7—Full flow
2—Right side
2—Split end post

Drop Back

5—Drop back
5—Split flow, 5 steps
4—Quarterback set up to right
0—Flare

5—Drop back
5—Split flow, 5 steps
5—Quarterback set up to left
0—Flare

A complete table of the pass routes we code is shown in Table 5-2.

The routes represented in this table are not drawn because of likely differences in terminology but we have found the system to be flexible and efficient.

Now that we have given an overview of coding the passing plays, let's look at our one passing play from Chapter 4—a drop back pass with split flow with the fullback running a flare route as the intended receiver. This play would be coded as 5550. An interpretation has already been given under coding the passing plays.

FINALIZED OFFENSIVE SCOUTING FORM

Refer to the completed offensive scouting form for our four sample plays (Form 5-2). In the next chapter we will discuss how to store the data in the computer now that it is in a form which can be processed.

SPECIAL SITUATIONS

Any computerized scouting system may at times be stretched to the limit of its capabilities. Generally, the equipment itself is not at fault, and the weakness lies with the ingenuity of the user. This has happened twice since we began using a personal computer. The first time occurred when one of our opponents used 11 different options out of a split back alignment; and the second time occurred when another of our opponents used six different called blocking schemes to the split end side of their pro I set versus our reduced Eagle defense. We knew that to stop each opponent, we would have to put special emphasis on these schemes. With the option offense we were able to use the following numbers to code each individual play differently in order to achieve discrete tendencies on each (Table 5-3):

TABLE 5-2

0 flare (right)	.3 flare (left half)	
.1 screen right	.8 HB pass	
.2 double pass		
1 flag	1.3 slot flag	1.6 wing flag
1.1 sideline and up	1.4 TE flag	1.7 curl and go
1.2 post corner	1.5 dart flag	
2 SE post	2.3 PB post	2.6 slot post
2.1 pipe	2.4 dart post	2.7 PB flag
2.2 seam post	2.5 wing post	
3 SE streak	3.3 TE post	3.6 PB streak
3.1 rail	3.4 slot streak	3.7 dark streak
3.2 TE rail	3.5 TE streak	3.8 wing streak
4 wheel flat	4.3 come back	4.6 HB delay
4.1 SE sideline	4.4 PB quick streak	4.7 SE delay
4.2 PB bench	4.5 rail out	4.8 corkscrew, stop
5 wheel	5.3 QB wheel	5.6 PB curl
5.1 SE slant	5.4 hang	5.7 PB slant
5.2 slot slant	5.5 wing hook	
6 TE across (drag)	6.3 middle screen	6.6 slot drag
6.1 TE delay	6.4 wheel drag	6.7 dive drag
6.2 rim drag	6.5 wing drag	6.8 PB drag
		6.9 SE drag
7 rim	7.3 QB rim	7.6 under
7.1 SE curl	7.4 TE curl	7.7 slot curl
7.2 dump	7.5 TE square in	7.8 wing dump
		7.9 trick
8 rim flat	8.3 switch	8.6 slot flat
8.1 hitch	8.4 PB quick out	8.7 TE out
8.2 TE flat	8.5 flood	8.8 corkscrew
		8.9 slam release, TE flat
9 swing	9.3 hitch and pitch	9.6 PB hang
9.1 screen left	9.4 SE hang	
9.2 swing (right half)	9.5 slot hang	

FORM 5-2

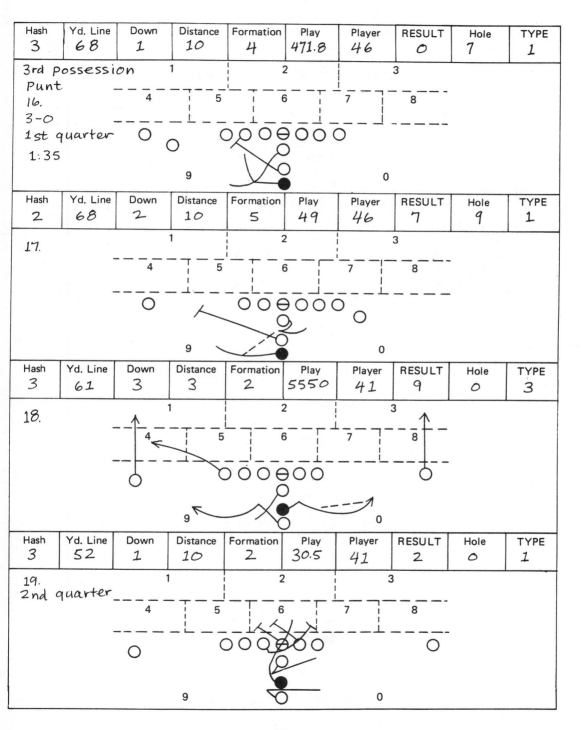

Hash	Yd. Line	Down	Distance	Formation	Play	Player	RESULT	Hole	TYPE
3	68	1	10	4	471.8	46	0	7	1

3rd possession
Punt
16.
3-0
1st quarter
1:35

Hash	Yd. Line	Down	Distance	Formation	Play	Player	RESULT	Hole	TYPE
2	68	2	10	5	49	46	7	9	1

17.

Hash	Yd. Line	Down	Distance	Formation	Play	Player	RESULT	Hole	TYPE
3	61	3	3	2	5550	41	9	0	3

18.

Hash	Yd. Line	Down	Distance	Formation	Play	Player	RESULT	Hole	TYPE
3	52	1	10	2	30.5	41	2	0	1

19.
2nd quarter

TABLE 5-3

OPTION OFFENSE—SPLIT BACKS		
Play	**Code (Right Only)**	**Diagram**
Inside veer	341 342 343	5-12
Zone veer	3612.2 3622.2 3632.2	5-13
Outside veer	361 362 363	5-14
Counter option	181 182 183	5-15
Misdirection option	351 352 353	5-16
Load option	2829 2839	5-17
Lead option	2828 2838	5-18
Whirlybird option	282 283	5-19
Speed option	2820 2830	5-20
Crazy option	382 383	5-21
Trap option	381.5 382.5 383.5	5-22

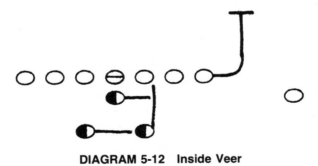

DIAGRAM 5-12   Inside Veer

DIAGRAM 5-13   Zone Veer

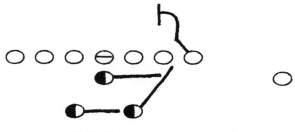

DIAGRAM 5-14   Outside Veer

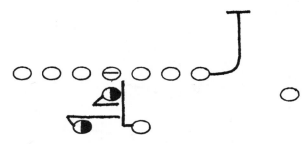

DIAGRAM 5-15   Counter Option

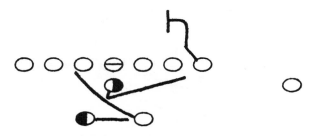

DIAGRAM 5-16   Misdirection Option

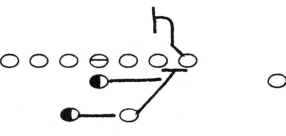

DIAGRAM 5-17   Load Option

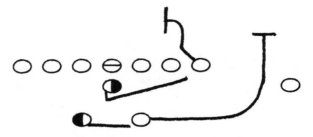

DIAGRAM 5-18   Lead Option

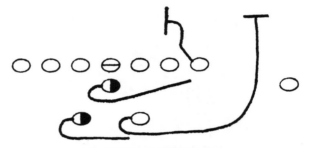

DIAGRAM 5-19   Whirlybird Option

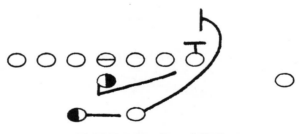

DIAGRAM 5-20   Speed Option

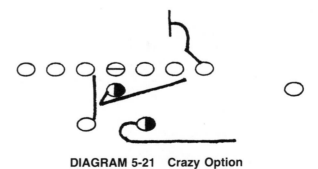

DIAGRAM 5-21   Crazy Option

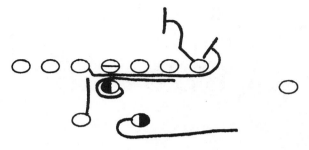

DIAGRAM 5-22 Trap Option

With the "called" blocking schemes we were able to use the following numbers to code each individual play differently in order to achieve discrete tendencies on each (Table 5-4).

TABLE 5-4

Play	Code (Left Only)	Diagram
Base	4910 4920 4930	5-23
G-pull	491.7 492.7 493.7	5-24
Down	4913.1 4923.1 4943.1	5-25
Load	4919 4929 4939	5-26
Combo	491.2 492.2 493.2	5-27
Log	4912.1 4922.1 4932.1	5-28

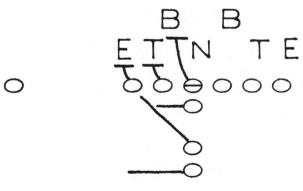

DIAGRAM 5-23 Base

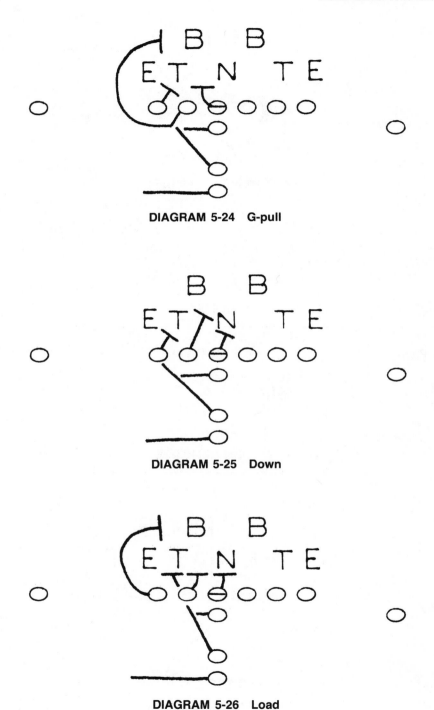

DIAGRAM 5-24   G-pull

DIAGRAM 5-25   Down

DIAGRAM 5-26   Load

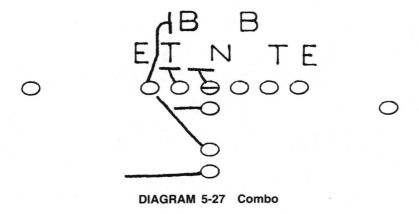

DIAGRAM 5-27   Combo

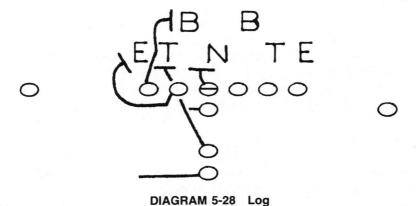

DIAGRAM 5-28   Log

CHAPTER 6

STORING THE DATA

In the preceding two chapters we walked you through the completion of the offensive scouting forms using four plays in one possession as our example. This established our data base. In scouting an actual opponent, you would record about 60 plays per game, and close to 200 over three games. This gives you enough of a data base to analyze your opponent's tendencies.

We have been mostly talking football over the last four chapters. Now we're going to talk computers again. Specifically, we will discuss a typical example of how, in about 20 minutes per game scouted, you can enter your raw data into the computer, have the computer check your data for input errors, store your data on a diskette, and begin analyzing your opponent's tendencies in order to develop your game plan to counter those tendencies. We will refer to our four plays along the way as we first describe the use of the keyboard.

THROUGH THE KEYBOARD

The first thing that we need to do is get our computer up and running. Most modern personal computers have instructions for automatic start stored in ROM (Read Only Memory). The only thing that we need to do is insert the diskette which contains our football scouting program into the disk drive (Photos 6-1 through 6-4) and turn on the power. We will then be greeted with a message that assures us that everything is

working properly and the computer is ready to accept the football
scouting program. A typical message of this type might be as follows:

MASTER DISKETTE CREATED ON 64K SYSTEM
DOS 3.3
ALAN B. HATFIELD
22 JUN 83

PHOTO 6-1

PHOTO 6-2

PHOTO 6-3

PHOTO 6-4

Notice that the message gives the type of diskette, the size of the memory of the system on which the diskette was created, the version of the disk operating system used, the owner of the diskette, and the date it was created. This administrative information should also appear on a label attached to the outside of the diskette for convenience.

The next step is to determine what is stored on the diskette. This is done by typing CATALOG and hitting the RETURN key. A typical display for a diskette on which the football scouting program has been stored might be as follows:

DISK VOLUME 254
A 002 HELLO
A 033 SCOUT

The volume of the diskette is given at the top. The two sets of instructions or files which have already been stored on this diskette are named HELLO and SCOUT. The first file displayed the original information on the screen when we turned on the computer. The second file is our football scouting program. The letter A is a symbol for the language in which the programs are written. In Chapter 11 we present a brief discussion of languages and programs. The numbers 002 and 033 give the numbers of sectors on the diskette that have been used to store each file. A sector is a small area on the diskette where information may be stored.

Next, we must instruct the computer to take the football scouting program, which is presently only on the diskette in the disk drive, and load it into RAM (Random Access Memory) inside the computer. We also want it to run the program so that we may begin storing our plays. This is done by typing RUN SCOUT and hitting the RETURN key. We are now greeted with the following:

IF YOU WISH TO INPUT PLAYS, PRESS X

Since our football scouting program is now stored in the computer but without any plays to be analyzed, we follow the instructions and press the key marked X. We are greeted with a flashing cursor (box) which tells us the computer is ready to accept our raw data from the offensive scouting forms. Each set of ten pieces of information from the offensive scouting form (Table 6-1) goes on a separate numbered line as a DATA statement with each piece of information separated from the next with a comma. After the line number, the word DATA, and our ten pieces of information from the offensive scouting form have been typed, we hit the RETURN key. This enters the data into the memory of the computer and readies the computer to accept the next line. After entering 20 plays the screen on the monitor would look like this:

1 DATA 1,89,1,10,2,43,22,0,3,1
2 DATA 1,89,2,10,5,48,22,0,8,1

```
3 DATA 2,89,3,10,2,4714.2, 42, 0, 4, 2
4 DATA 1,70,1,10,6,49,22,13,9,1
5 DATA 1,57,1,10,6,3458.9,41,14,8,3
6 DATA 3,43,1,10,2,5550,41,0,0,2
7 DATA 3,43,2,10,1,49.1,22,9,9,1
8 DATA 2,34,3,1,4,48,22,9,8,1
9 DATA 3,25,1,10,4,3458.8,41,11,8,3
10 DATA 3,15,1,10,2,48.1,22,3,8,1
11 DATA 3,12,2,7,2,4714.2, 81,0,4,2
12 DATA 3,12,3,7,2,31.5,41,2,1,1
13 DATA 2,80,1,10,1,49.1,46,5,9,1
14 DATA 1,75,2,5,6,3456.9,82,0,6,2
15 DATA 1,75,3,5,2,3476,82,12,6,3
16 DATA 3,68,1,10,4,471.8,46,0,7,1
17 DATA 2,68,2,10,5,49,46,7,9,1
18 DATA 3,61,3,3,2,5550,41,9,0,3
19 DATA 3,52,1,10,2,30.5,41,2,0,1
20 DATA 3,50,2,8,4,48,46,3,8,1
```

TABLE 6-1   Offensive Scouting Form

You may recognize plays 16 to 19 as being those used in Chapters 4 and 5 when we discussed the completion of the offensive scouting form (Form 5-2).

ON THE DISKETTE

Once all the plays have been entered, we must store the football scouting program that includes the plays to be analyzed on the diskette for future reference. This is accomplished by typing SAVE KATY where SAVE is an instruction to the computer and KATY is the name of our opponent being scouted. Hitting the RETURN key accomplishes two things: It places the information on our opponent on the diskette and it adds a file named KATY to the catalog. If we did not save our information and the power went off, everything in RAM would be lost— football scouting program and the plays just typed. We can check to see if a new file has been added to our diskette by typing CATALOG and hitting the RETURN key. We will be greeted with the following:

```
DISK VOLUME 254

A 002 HELLO
A 033 SCOUT
A 056 KATY
```

All is well, and we are ready to start analyzing our opponent.

SELF-CHECK SYSTEM

To analyze the data we again type RUN and the computer runs the program in memory. We need not add the word KATY because it is the *only* program in memory. We are again greeted with the following as the computer runs the program:

IF YOU WISH TO INPUT PLAYS, PRESS X

We have input all the plays, so we hit any other key than X and are greeted with the following:

PLEASE REMEMBER—YOU MUST CHECK THE PLAYS ONLY
AT THE BEGINNING OF EACH RUN
I SHALL CHECK THE PLAYS

The computer is telling us that it has been programmed to catch our typing errors. These errors could include a fifth down, a deleted play, a jersey number over 99, an unacceptable hole number, or a misplaced comma. If we have made such a mistake the computer will catch it and instruct us as to which line or lines need to be retyped and restored on the diskette. If all is well, we will see the following message in a matter of seconds:

ALL PLAYS ARE IN THE CORRECT FORM
HIT A KEY WHEN YOU ARE READY TO GO ON

We hit a key and the following appears:

1 = TOTAL SUMMARY OF ALL SITUATIONS
2 = TOTAL OF LEFT AND RIGHT HASH SITUATIONS
3 = TOTAL OF EACH FORMATION
4 = FORMATION BREAKDOWN BY HASHMARKS
5 = TOTAL DOWN AND DISTANCE SITUATIONS
6 = DOWN AND DISTANCE BREAKDOWN BY HASHMARKS
  AND DIFFERENT FIELD ZONES
7 = GAME AND INDIVIDUAL STATISTICS
WHICH NUMBER DO YOU WISH TO SEE?

Now we're back to talking football. Well, not immediately. We will take a look at where we go from here in the next chapter. First, we need to talk computers one last time, but we will be discussing three extremely important topics. Those topics are error messages, initialization of diskettes, and back-up copies.

ERROR MESSAGES

Fortunately for us, the computer has been programmed to catch the mistakes we make as we interact with the computer. These mistakes are communicated to us by error messages. These messages are of the following four varieties:

1. Mistakes made as an instruction is being typed.
2. Mistakes made when a program is being executed.
3. Mistakes made when an input statement is being responded to.
4. Mistakes made when the disk drive is being used.

The most common error message that will be displayed while typing instructions is SYNTAX ERROR. In this case something has been typed that the computer does not understand or cannot accept. It may be as simple as typing the letter O when you mean the number 0, or misspelling the words CATALOG or RUN. Syntax error messages are always easy to correct. Just retype what you really mean.

The second variety occurs when the program is being executed. An OUT OF MEMORY ERROR message is an example. If you have loaded a program with more data than can be manipulated by the memory installed in your computer, this error message will be displayed. Entering too many plays, too many different formations, or consistently coding too much information per play may cause the available memory to be stretched beyond its limit. This can be corrected by economizing your coding or dividing the plays you store in separate files. Another type of error with the same solution is the DIVISION BY ZERO ERROR. We won't elaborate on how this actually comes about. We will just mention that too much data has overloaded the computer, and it is letting us know. If you attempt to run the SCOUT program with too few plays, you may also get the DIVISION BY ZERO ERROR.

The next error message occurs when you are responding to an input statement and type something that was not expected. An example could be if you typed a letter when a number was expected, or a number that was not one of the options listed. In this case a RETYPE LINE message will be displayed and the cure is to do just what it says.

The fourth variety of error message will be displayed when using the disk drive. An I/O ERROR, which means input-output error, may be displayed if you request data from the disk drive and the door isn't shut. Simply turn your system off and start over. Never close the door when the red light of the drive is on. That will wipe out sections of your diskette. If you misspell a file name or ask for a file that is not present on a given diskette, the FILE NOT FOUND message will be displayed. Again, retype or replace the diskette with the one that contains the program you want.

We have discussed some typical error messages. Most computer operators will be confronted with them sooner or later. These messages are simply reminders that something has gone wrong and must be corrected for the program and equipment to operate properly. Different manufacturers of hardware using different languages or various versions of the same language may use slightly different terms for their error messages. The best reference source is the user's manual for the hardware, or the programmer's manual for the software that comes with your computer (Chapter 11). These manuals should become an easily accessible part of your permanent computer library.

INITIALIZING DISKETTES

When you purchase a new diskette, it is blank. You must therefore initialize or format the diskette so that it is capable of starting up, booting, your personal computer, and may be used for the storage of information. This information is stored on the diskette in small areas called sectors. The new diskette is first divided into these sectors by using a system master diskette which comes with your hardware, and then following a prescribed procedure which is outlined in the user's manual for your particular disk operating system; the necessary instructions are added. Once your new diskette has been intialized, it may be used for storing information.

MAKING BACK-UP COPIES

It is always wise to have two copies of all your important diskettes such as the system master and your football scouting diskette. Your user's manual for the disk operating system will outline how to copy an entire diskette onto a new diskette. That way you'll always have a back-up should disaster strike (cats, dogs, heat, kids, magnetic objects, etc.) and your original is wiped out.

Diskettes may be copy-protected. This means that the instructions have been placed on the diskette in such a way that they can't be transferred to a new diskette, or if they can be transferred, the instructions won't work anyway. This of course prevents the unauthorized use of the diskette and its contents. If you purchase a football scouting diskette whose instructions are copy-protected, make sure that you are supplied with a back-up in case something happens to the original.

CHAPTER 7

DISPLAYING THE DATA

We are now back to talking football as we display our data base and interpret the charts. In the next few chapters we will put our computer data base to work as we analyze the tendencies of our opponent, devise a game plan, and implement our strategy. When we last discussed our computerized scouting system, the monitor was displaying the following:

```
1 = TOTAL SUMMARY OF ALL SITUATIONS
2 = TOTAL OF LEFT AND RIGHT HASH SITUATIONS
3 = TOTAL OF EACH FORMATION
4 = FORMATION BREAKDOWN BY HASHMARKS
5 = TOTAL DOWN AND DISTANCE SITUATIONS
6 = DOWN AND DISTANCE BREAKDOWN BY HASHMARKS
    AND DIFFERENT FIELD ZONES
7 = GAME AND INDIVIDUAL STATISTICS
    WHICH NUMBER DO YOU WISH TO SEE?
```

We will now follow the computer's lead as we interpret the four basic charts of our computerized scouting system under the total summary of all situations. These charts are as follows:

1. Passing Zones
2. The Passing Plays
3. The Hole Chart
4. The Running Plays

We will then take a look at the last category which is Game and Individual Statistics.

PASSING ZONES

We first need an overview of our opponent's offense. This is accomplished by 1 = TOTAL SUMMARY OF ALL SITUATIONS. We type a 1 in response to the question on the screen and hit the RETURN key. The computer asks the following:

ARE THESE DEFENSES OR OFFENSES? (1 = DEFENSE, 2 = OFFENSE)

We type a 2 and hit the RETURN key. The computer asks the following:

DO YOU WANT A PRINTOUT? (Y/N)

We type a Y for yes and hit the RETURN key. The computer tells us the following:

THE TOTAL SUMMARY IS COMING

Within a few seconds, the following chart is displayed on the monitor and printed on paper (Printout 7-1):

```
┌─────────────────────────────────────────────┐
│     THE TOTAL SUMMARY OF...                   │
│            PASSING ZONES                      │
│ ********************************************* │
│                                               │
│                                               │
│         5        3       7                    │
│                                               │
│ 6       6       15       7       11           │
│                                               │
│         -----o o o o o-----                   │
│                   o                           │
│         2                6                    │
│READY                                          │
└─────────────────────────────────────────────┘
```

PRINTOUT 7-1

This is the passing zones chart which has been computed using entries from the hole (zone) and type categories on our offensive scouting form. This indicates the number of passes thrown into each of the zones numbered 0 through 9 on the offensive scouting form. Notice that the chart is tabulated from the offense's point of view. The READY means that the computer has computed the next chart. By hitting a key, the next chart will be displayed and printed.

THE PASSING PLAYS

Upon hitting a key after the READY message is given, the computer gives us the passing plays chart which is computed using entries from the play, result, and type categories on our offensive scouting form. This chart breaks the passing game down into play action (3000 series), sprint out (4700 series), and drop back passes (5500 series) with corresponding routes and blocking schemes at the discretion of the person who coded the original plays. For the sake of example we have included an abbreviated chart with a description of each play added to the right in Printout 7-2. The statistical breakdown of each individual pass includes attempts, completions, percent of times attempted as compared to total attempts (% ATTEM), and total yards for completions (TOT YD). This chart gives an overview of the specifics of the opponent's passing game.

Note that the drop back pass coded 5550 was thrown more (four times) than any other. We will continue to use this pass as one of our examples as we track our four specific plays in the next chapter. If we continue to follow the computer's lead and HIT A KEY, the next chart will be displayed and printed when we are ready.

THE HOLE CHART

We now move to our opponent's running game. Upon hitting a key the following chart is displayed (Printout 7-3):

This is the hole chart which has been computed by using entries from the result, hole, and type categories on the offensive scouting form. It is drawn from the offense's point of view. It gives the number of times the offense attacked each hole (FREQ), the percent of total runs that attacked each hole (PRCT), and the total yards gained at each point of attack (T.YD).

Additional information represented on the hole chart includes the total number of passes thrown (68), the percent of passes as compared to total plays (38%), the percent of running plays to the left or odd-numbered holes (46%), and the percent of running plays to the right or even-numbered holes (53%). Again the computer gives us a READY message when it has finished computing the next chart.

THE RUNNING PLAYS

The next chart itemizes the running plays. It is computed using entries from the play, result and type categories on the offensive scouting

THE PASSING PLAYS					Play Action
PASS/ATTEMPTS/COMPLETIONS/%ATTEM/TOT YD					
3436	1	0	1	0	iso, TE across
3441.8	1	0	1	0	power, flag, waggle
3444.9	1	1	1	14	power, wheel flat, bootleg
3446.9	1	0	1	0	power, SE drag
3456.8	1	0	1	0	power, PB drag
3456.9	2	0	2	0	power, SE drag
3458.8	3	1	4	11	power, corkscrew
3458.9	2	1	2	14	power, slam release, TE flat
3462.3	1	1	1	23	sprint draw, PB post
3465.6	1	0	1	0	sprint draw, PB curl
3466	2	2	2	18	sprint draw, TE across

---MORE TO FOLLOW---
READY
?

3474	1	0	1	0	sprint draw, wheel flat
3475.4	2	1	2	17	sprint draw, hang
3476	2	2	2	13	sprint draw, TE across
3476.9	1	0	1	0	sprint draw, SE drag
3478.2	1	0	1	0	sprint draw, TE flat
3485.7	1	0	1	0	sweep, PB slant
					Sprint Out Left
4713.6	1	0	1	0	PB streak
4713.8	1	1	1	30	wing streak
4714.2	3	1	4	11	PB bench
4715	2	1	2	21	wheel
4715.6	1	1	1	18	PB curl
4717.2	1	0	1	0	dump

---MORE TO FOLLOW---

					Sprint Out Right
4722.7	1	0	1	0	PB flag
4724.1	2	0	2	0	SE sideline
4724.2	2	0	2	0	PB bench
4726.1	1	1	1	10	TE delay
4727	1	1	1	16	rim
4727.2	1	1	1	6	dump
4728	1	1	1	6	rim flat
4728.5	1	0	1	0	flood
					Drop Back Right
5540	2	2	2	12	flare
5543.1	1	1	1	62	rail
5543.6	1	1	1	35	PB streak
5544.6	1	0	1	0	HB delay
5545.4	1	0	1	0	hang
5546.4	1	1	1	8	wheel drag
5547.4	1	0	1	0	TE curl
					Drop Back Left
5550	4	2	5	22	flare
5551.4	1	0	1	0	TE flag
5553	3	0	4	0	SE streak
5553.5	1	0	1	0	TE streak
5553.6	1	0	1	0	PB streak
5556	1	0	1	0	TE across
5556.8	1	1	1	4	PB drag
5557.1	1	0	1	0	SE curl
5557.4	1	1	1	15	TE curl
5558.8	1	1	1	19	corkscrew
5559	1	1	1	10	swing
5559.1	1	1	1	-7	screen left

PRINTOUT 7-3

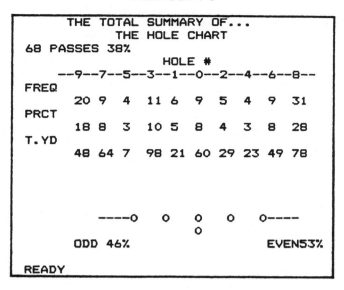

form. For the sake of example we have included an abbreviated chart with description of each play added to the right as seen in Printout 7-4. The running plays are broken down by the number of times each was executed (FREQ), the percent of total runs (PRCT), the total yards gained (TOT.YDS), and the average yards per play (AVG.YDS). We will use the runs coded 30.5, 49, and 471.8 as the other three plays in our four-play example. We have chosen to track these three in addition to the 5550 pass because of the following:

1. We have used them as our examples in previous chapters.
2. They were all run a significant number of times (seven, ten, and nine times, respectively) over the three games we have scouted.
3. They were all run for significant total yardage (44, 48, and 70 yards, respectively).
4. They each had a significant yards per carry—AVG. YDS.— (six, four, and seven, respectively) over the three games we have scouted.
5. They were run in a four-play sequence with pass 5550 in the first game scouted. (See Chapter 6, Table 1, Plays 16-19)

```
THE RUNNING PLAYS

PLAY--FREQ--PRCT-TOT.YDS--AVG.YDS
10       1     0     0        0        QB sneak

30.5     7     3     44       6        FB trap

31.5     5     2     25       5        FB trap

34       4     2     23       5        FB veer

35       3     1     12       4        FB veer

43       9     5     16       1        isolation

48       12    6     23       1        sweep

48.1     6     3     39       6        sweep, crack

49       10    5     48       4        sweep

49.1     3     1     12       4        sweep, crack

301.9    1     0     16       16       FB draw

           ---MORE TO FOLLOW---

HIT A KEY WHEN YOU ARE READY
311.9    1     0     -4       -4       FB draw

321.9    1     0     0        0        FB draw

325      3     1     20       6        FB counter

331.9    2     1     82       41       FB draw

342      1     0     0        0        veer, QB keep

347      1     0     -7       -7       FB trick

461.8    7     3     48       6        sprint draw

465.5    2     1     1        0        I back counter, G trap

471      2     1     -7       -4       I back off tackle

471.8    9     5     70       7        sprint draw

472      1     0     -6       -6       I back off tackle, QB keep

474      1     0     12       12       I back off tackle, F block

           ---MORE TO FOLLOW---

HIT A KEY WHEN YOU ARE READY
```

PRINTOUT 7-4 continued

475.5	3	1	11	3	I back counter, G trap
483.8	1	0	15	15	waggle, pitch
554	2	1	−16	−8	scramble, drop back
555	2	1	−12	−6	scramble, drop back
3458.8	1	0	−5	−5	scramble, play action
3465.4	1	0	−5	−5	scramble, play action
3468	1	0	−1	−1	scramble, play action
3480	1	0	−1	−1	scramble, play action
4828	1	0	6	6	lead option, QB keep
4838	1	0	10	10	lead option, pitch
4838.1	2	1	8	4	lead option, pitch, crack
READY					

When we are ready to continue, we hit a key and the following is displayed:

    1 = TOTAL SUMMARY OF ALL SITUATIONS
    2 = TOTAL LEFT AND RIGHT HASH SITUATIONS
    3 = TOTAL OF EACH FORMATION
    4 = FORMATION BREAKDOWN BY HASHMARKS
    5 = TOTAL DOWN AND DISTANCE SITUATIONS
    6 = DOWN AND DISTANCE BREAKDOWN BY HASHMARKS
        AND DIFFERENT FIELD ZONES
    7 = GAME AND INDIVIDUAL STATISTICS
    WHICH NUMBER DO YOU WISH TO SEE?

It is now our option to further break down our opponent by hash, formation, formation by hashmarks, down and distance, or a combination of down and distance by hashmarks and field zones. We will still have the four charts previously discussed displayed, but now the criteria for analysis have become more selective as we use breakdown numbers 2 to 6. We will discuss each of these using our four selected plays as an example in the next chapter.

GAME AND INDIVIDUAL STATISTICS

The readout 7 = GAME AND INDIVIDUAL STATISTICS is computed using entries from the player, result, and type categories. It also uses a different format for displaying the information. The four areas in which information is presented are as follows:

1. The Rushing Game by Individual Player
2. Team Rushing Statistics
3. The Passing Game by Individual Receiver
4. Team Passing Statistics

On the rushing game chart the players are listed by jersey number, total individual carries, percent of team carries, total individual yards, and average yards gained or lost (Printout 7-5).

```
            THE RUSHING GAME

PLAYER/CARRIES/%/TOT YDS/AVERAGE
********************************************
11        12      11     -47        -4

22        46      42     202         4

37        1       0      -1         -1

38        3       2      33         11

41        26      24     192         7

42        1       0      -5         -5

46        19      17     103         5
```

PRINTOUT 7-5

Team totals are listed in Printout 7-6.

On the passing game the receiver's jersey number is listed. Attempts, completions, percent of total attempts, and total yards in receptions are listed as seen in Printout 7-7.

Team totals are listed last in Printout 7-8.

PRINTOUT 7-6

TOTAL RUSHES	TOTALYARDS	AVERAGE
108	477	4.41666667

PRINTOUT 7-7

THE PASSING GAME**********

RECEIVER	ATTEMPTS	COMPL	%ATT	TOT YDS	
22	2	1		2	3
32	9	4		13	77
37	11	7		16	129
38	3	2		4	21
41	9	5		13	54
42	5	1		7	17
46	3	3		4	12
80	6	1		8	18
81	5	1		7	30
82	9	2		13	22
86	2	0		2	0

---MORE TO FOLLOW---

READY
?

| 88 | 4 | 2 | | 5 | 25 |

PRINTOUT 7-8

TOT ATMPT	TOTCOMP	%COMP	AVG YDS
68	29	42	6

As you have no doubt begun to realize, there is a wealth of information at the fingertips of the coach. Only a few strokes of the keys on the personal computer will bring it all to the coach's attention. In the next chapter we will take a more in-depth look at the breakdown of our four sample plays.

CHAPTER **8**

BREAKING DOWN TENDENCIES

In Chapter 7 we discussed the four charts—passing zones, passing plays, hole chart, and running plays—under the total summary of all situations. From this overview of our opponent's offense we have chosen to track one pass (5550) and three runs (30.5, 49, and 471.8) through the following:

>   2 = TOTAL OF LEFT AND RIGHT HASH SITUATIONS
>   3 = TOTAL OF EACH FORMATION
>   4 = FORMATION BREAKDOWN BY HASHMARKS
>   5 = TOTAL DOWN AND DISTANCE SITUATIONS
>   6 = DOWN AND DISTANCE BREAKDOWN BY HASHMARKS
>   AND DIFFERENT FIELD ZONES

BY HASHMARKS

Typing 2 = TOTAL OF LEFT AND RIGHT HASH SITUATIONS will display our four charts, but it will sort the data into left and right hashmarks only. We will begin to see strong tendencies surfacing from our computer data base as we scan the charts. By selecting breakdown 2 and following the computer's lead as we did in the previous chapter, the first chart that is displayed is as follows (Printout 8-1). The obvious conclusion is that when our opponent is on the left hashmark, passes into the middle hook (zone 6) and flat area to the field (zone 8) predominate with seven attempts each. We will make a mental note of this tendency for future reference while previewing the other breakdowns.

PRINTOUT 8-1

```
TOTALS FOR LEFT HASH
            PASSING ZONES
*****************************************

            1           1           1

 O          1           7           2           7

            ------o o o o o------
                        o
            o                       o
READY
```

The next chart we will consider is the hole chart (Printout 8-2).

PRINTOUT 8-2

```
TOTALS FOR LEFT HASH
            THE HOLE CHART
20 PASSES 37%
                    HOLE #
    --9--7--5--3--1--0--2--4--6--8--
FREQ
     6  1  2  2  1  3  3  1  3  11
PRCT
     18 3  6  6  3  9  9  3  9  33
T.YD
     41 3  2  1  12 20 10 3  20 10



            ----o   o   o   o   o----
                        o
    ODD 36%                      EVEN63%
```

Our opponent not only has a strong tendency to throw to the field from the left hashmark, but he also has a strong tendency to run to the field which would be to his right or toward the even-numbered holes (63%). The majority of those runs (11) have attacked the 8 hole. He has gained good yardage (41) going back to the boundary. We will take a closer look at this with the running plays.

The next chart lists the running plays (Printout 8-3).

```
THE RUNNING PLAYS

PLAY--FREQ--PRCT-TOT.YDS--AVG.YDS
10        1     1     0        0

30.5      1     1     4        4

31.5      1     1    12       12

34        1     1     3        3

35        1     1     7        7

43        2     3     1        0

48        2     3    -5       -3

49        6    11    41        6

301.9     1     1    16       16

321.9     1     1     0        0

325       2     3    10        5

        ---MORE TO FOLLOW---

HIT A KEY WHEN YOU ARE READY
342       1     1     0        0

461.8     3     5    20        6

472       1     1    -6       -6

475.5     2     3     9        4

483.8     1     1    15       15

554       1     1    -6       -6

3465.4 1        1    -5       -5

3468      1     1    -1       -1

3480      1     1    -1       -1

4838.1 2        3     8        4
```

88

We immediately see a tendency to run 49 six out of ten times (see total summary, running plays) when the ball is on the left hashmark. This one play accounts for all 41 yards at the 9 hole as depicted on the hole chart. As we prepare our game plan, we will keep this in mind.

The computer now moves us over to the right hashmark (Printout 8-4).

PRINTOUT 8-4

```
┌─────────────────────────────────────────────────────┐
│         THE TOTALS FOR RIGHT HASH                     │
│             PASSING ZONES                             │
│  ********************************************          │
│                                                       │
│         4          1          3                       │
│                                                       │
│   4     3          6          2          3            │
│                                                       │
│         ------o o o o o-----                          │
│                       o                               │
│              o               3                        │
└─────────────────────────────────────────────────────┘
```

Our opponent's passing attack is much more balanced from the right hashmark than it was from the left hashmark. They have begun to use some flare control into the boundary. Notice the three attempts behind the line of scrimmage into the 0 zone.

Let's check to see what pass is actually being thrown into the 0 zone on the next chart (Printout 8-5). It is our 5550 example which was the pass attempted most often (three times).

Looking at the running tendencies on the right hash, we start with the following as seen on Printout 8-6. Again, a tendency toward a more balanced attack (52% - 47%) is evident, but running wide into the boundary predominates (26%). Good yardage has been gained (51) at the 7 hole and gained (90) at the 3 hole.

The list of the running plays gives us further insight as seen in Printout 8-7.

We will again reserve our comments for our sample plays. Play 30.5 has been run four of its seven times from the right hashmark for a nine yard average. Play 471.8 has been run eight of its nine times for a seven yard average. Notice on the hole chart that at hole 7 a frequency of only seven was recorded. This is because the runner bounced the play outside one time and the hole number was recorded as 9. This type of information can lead to important coaching points on the practice field.

THE PASSING PLAYS

PASS/ATTEMPTS/COMPLETIONS/%ATTEM/TOT YD

PASS	ATTEMPTS	COMPLETIONS	%ATTEM	TOT YD
3436	1	O	3	O
3444.9	1	1	3	14
3446.9	1	O	3	O
3456.8	1	O	3	O
3458.8	2	1	6	11
3474	1	O	3	O
3475.4	1	O	3	O
3476	1	1	3	1
3476.9	1	O	3	O
3478.2	1	O	3	O
4713.8	1	1	3	30

---MORE TO FOLLOW---
READY
?

PASS	ATTEMPTS	COMPLETIONS	%ATTEM	TOT YD
4714.2	1	O	3	O
4715	2	1	6	21
4715.6	1	1	3	18
4717.2	1	O	3	O
4722.7	1	O	3	O
4728	1	1	3	6
5550	3	1	10	9
5551.4	1	O	3	O
5553	2	O	6	O
5556	1	O	3	O
5556.8	1	1	3	4
5557.1	1	O	3	O

---MORE TO FOLLOW---
READY
?
| 5558.8 | 1 | 1 | 3 | 19 |

PRINTOUT 8-6

```
+-------------------------------------------------------+
|          THE  TOTALS  FOR  RIGHT  HASH                |
|             THE  HOLE  CHART                          |
|  29 PASSES 38%                                        |
|                          HOLE #                       |
|        --9--7--5--3--1--0--2--4--6--8--               |
|  FREQ                                                 |
|         8   7   1   6   2   4   1   2   3   12        |
|  PRCT                                                 |
|        17  15  2  13   4   8   2   4   6   26         |
|  T.YD                                                 |
|         0  51   0  90  -2  36   9  17  19  19         |
|                                                       |
|                                                       |
|              ----o    o    o    o    o----            |
|                             o                         |
|        ODD 52%                         EVEN47%        |
+-------------------------------------------------------+
```

BY FORMATION

We now move to 3 = TOTAL OF EACH FORMATION. We will only consider the formations from which our sample plays were run a significant number of times and the relevant charts. We have our formations coding key for reference as needed (Printout 8-8).

Play 5550 has only been run (four of four) from formation 2 (I Pro Left Right End Split) with 22 total yards gained (Printout 8-9).

Play 30.5 has been run five out of seven times, and play 471.8 has been run six out of nine times from formation I Pro Left Right End Split with a five and seven yard average respectively (Printout 8-9).

Continuing through the formations we find the following (Printouts 8-10 and 8-11):

Our opponent ran left to the odd numbered holes 91% of the time in I Wing Left Right End Split (The Hole Chart, Printout 8-11). Play 49 was run 6 (The Running Plays, Formation I Wing Left Right End Split, Frequency Column, Printout 8-10) of 10 times (The Running Plays, The Total Summary, Frequency Column, Printout 7-4, Page 82) from I Wing Left Right End Split formation. This play accounted for 6 (The Running Plays, Formation I Wing Left Right End Split, Frequency Column, Printout 8-10) of the 8 times (The Hole Chart, Hole #9, Frequency Row, Printout 8-11) hole 9 was attacked and 23 (The Running Plays, Formation I Wing Left Right End Split, Total Yards Column, Printout 8-10) of the 37 yards gained (The Hole Chart, Hole #9, Total Yards Row, Printout 8-11).

PRINTOUT 8-7

```
THE RUNNING PLAYS

PLAY--FREQ--PRCT-TOT.YDS--AVG.YDS
30.5     4      5      36          9

31.5     1      1      2           2

34       2      2      17          8

35       1      1      0           0

43       4      5      8           2

48       7      9      13          1

48.1     4      5      11          2

49       1      1      2           2

49.1     1      1      9           9

311.9    1      1      -4          -4

331.9    2      2      82          41

          ---MORE TO FOLLOW---

HIT A KEY WHEN YOU ARE READY
347      1      1      -7          -7

461.8    1      1      18          18

465.5    2      2      1           0

471      1      1      -6          -6

471.8    8      10     60          7

474      1      1      12          12

475.5    1      1      2           2

555      2      2      -12         -6

3458.8   1      1      -5          -5
```

```
┌─────────────────┐
│ FORMATION 2     │
└─────────────────┘
```

```
┌──────────────────────────────────────────────┐
│ THE PASSING PLAYS                              │
│                                                │
│ PASS/ATTEMPTS/COMPLETIONS/%ATTEM/TOT YD        │
│ 3436      1         0         3       0        │
│                                                │
│ 3475.4    2         1         6       17       │
│                                                │
│ 3476      2         2         6       13       │
│                                                │
│ 3476.9    1         0         3       0        │
│                                                │
│ 3478.2    1         0         3       0        │
│                                                │
│ 4713.6    1         0         3       0        │
│                                                │
│ 4713.8    1         1         3       30       │
│                                                │
│ 4714.2    3         1         9       11       │
│                                                │
│ 4715      1         0         3       0        │
│                                                │
│ 4715.6    1         1         3       18       │
│                                                │
│ 4717.2    1         0         3       0        │
│                                                │
│         ---MORE TO FOLLOW---                   │
│ READY                                          │
│ ?                                              │
│ 5550      4         2         12      22       │
│                                                │
│ 5551.4    1         0         3       0        │
│                                                │
│ 5553      3         0         9       0        │
│                                                │
│ 5553.5    1         0         3       0        │
│                                                │
│ 5553.6    1         0         3       0        │
│                                                │
│ 5556      1         0         3       0        │
│                                                │
│ 5556.8    1         1         3       4        │
│                                                │
│ 5557.1    1         0         3       0        │
│                                                │
│ 5557.4    1         1         3       15       │
│                                                │
│ 5558.8    1         1         3       19       │
│                                                │
│ 5559      1         1         3       10       │
│                                                │
│ 5559.1    1         1         3       -7       │
└──────────────────────────────────────────────┘
```

PRINTOUT 8-9

```
THE RUNNING PLAYS

PLAY--FREQ--PRCT-TOT.YDS--AVG.YDS
30.5    5    7    28        5

31.5    1    1    2         2

34      1    1    3         3

35      1    1    0         0

43      5    7    10        2

48      1    1    0         0

48.1    6    8    39        6

311.9   1    1    -4        -4

325     2    2    16        8

331.9   2    2    82        41

471     2    2    -7        -4

        ---MORE TO FOLLOW---

HIT A KEY WHEN YOU ARE READY
471.8   6    8    45        7

555     2    2    -12       -6
```

PRINTOUT 8-10　I Wing Left Right End Split

```
THE RUNNING PLAYS

PLAY--FREQ--PRCT-TOT.YDS--AVG.YDS
35      2    11   12        6

49      6    33   23        3

474     1    5    12        12

475.5   3    16   11        3
```

PRINTOUT 8-11   I Wing Left Right End Split

```
FORMATION 6

              THE HOLE CHART
6 PASSES 33%
                   HOLE #
    --9--7--5--3--1--0--2--4--6--8--
FREQ
      8  1  2  0  0  0  0  0  0  1
PRCT
      66 8  16 0  0  0  0  0  0  8
T.YD
      37 3  12 0  0  0  0  0  0  6




         ----o  o  o  o  o----
                   o
    ODD 91%                    EVEN8%
```

BY FORMATIONS ON THE HASHMARKS

Combining the last two criteria, 4 = FORMATION BREAKDOWN BY
HASHMARKS gives us the following information on our four sample
plays (Printouts 8-12 through 8-15): play 49 was run from I Wing Left
Right End Split.

   If you have been following our discussion to this point, no further

PRINTOUT 8-12

```
FORMATION 2
ON THE RIGHT HASH

              PASSING ZONES
************************************

         3         1         2

2        3         4         2        0
         -----o o o o o-----
                   o
         o                   3
```

PRINTOUT 8-13

```
THE PASSING PLAYS

PASS/ATTEMPTS/COMPLETIONS/%ATTEM/TOT YD
3436        1         0          5       0

3475.4      1         0          5       0

3476        1         1          5       1

3476.9      1         0          5       0

3478.2      1         0          5       0

4713.8      1         1          5      30

4714.2      1         0          5       0

4715        1         0          5       0

4715.6      1         1          5      18

4717.2      1         0          5       0

5550        3         1         15       9

         ---MORE TO FOLLOW---
READY
?
5551.4      1         0          5       0

5553        2         0         10       0

5556        1         0          5       0

5556.8      1         1          5       4

5557.1      1         0          5       0

5558.8      1         1          5      19
```

PRINTOUT 8-14

```
FORMATION 2
ON THE RIGHT HASH

             THE HOLE CHART
20 PASSES 46%
                      HOLE #
    --9--7--5--3--1--0--2--4--6--8--
FREQ
     3   4  1   4  2  3  1  0   0  5
PRCT
     13 17  4  17  8 13  4  0   0 21
T.YD
     -1826 0  86 -2 24  9  0   0 11



          ----O   O   O   O   O----
                          O
      ODD 60%                 EVEN39%
```

PRINTOUT 8-15

```
THE RUNNING PLAYS

PLAY--FREQ--PRCT-TOT.YDS--AVG.YDS
 30.5   3     6     24        8

 31.5   1     2      2        2

 35     1     2      O        O

 43     2     4      4        2

 48     1     2      O        O

 48.1   4     9     11        2

 311.9  1     2     -4       -4

 331.9  2     4     82       41

 471    1     2     -6       -6

 471.8  5    11     35        7

 555    2     4    -12       -6
```

comments on the interpretation of the charts is necessary. The tendencies are obvious.

Our last example of formation on the hash marks is the play 49 run (Printouts 8-16 through 8-19).

(Again, we leave the interpretation to you.)

PRINTOUT 8-16

```
FORMATION 6
ON THE LEFT HASH
            THE HOLE CHART
5 PASSES 45%
                    HOLE #
   --9--7--5--3--1--0--2--4--6--8--
FREQ
    3  1  1  0  0  0  0  0  0  1
PRCT
    50 16 16 0  0  0  0  0  0  16
T.YD
    18 3  7  0  0  0  0  0  0  6



        ----0   0   0   0   0----
                        0
    ODD 83%                  EVEN16%
```

PRINTOUT 8-17

```
THE RUNNING PLAYS

PLAY--FREQ--PRCT-TOT.YDS--AVG.YDS
35      1    9    7         7

49      3    27   18        6

475.5  2    18   9          4
```

PRINTOUT 8-18

```
FORMATION 6
IN THE MIDDLE
NO PASSES HERE
READY
FORMATION 6
IN THE MIDDLE
          THE HOLE CHART
NO PASSES
                    HOLE #
     --9--7--5--3--1--0--2--4--6--8--
FREQ
       3   0   1   0   0   0   0   0   0   0
PRCT
       75  0   25  0   0   0   0   0   0   0
T.YD
       5   0   5   0   0   0   0   0   0   0



            ----o    o    o    o    o----
                            o
     ODD 100%                        EVENO%
```

PRINTOUT 8-19

```
THE RUNNING PLAYS

PLAY--FREQ--PRCT-TOT.YDS--AVG.YDS
35      1      25     5         5

49      3      75     5         1
```

BY DOWN AND DISTANCE

Punching in 5 = TOTAL DOWN AND DISTANCE SITUATIONS gives us tendencies for long (seven–ten yards), medium (three–six yards), and short (zero–two yards) situations by down. We will use first down and long yardage as our example (Printouts 8-20 through 8-23).

Our opponent has used the 5550 pass (three of four) predominantly on first down. He has thrown the ball 40 percent of the time. He has run wide at holes 8 and 9 49 percent of the time (28% + 21%). He has used the 49 run (five times) more than any other play in this situation for a seven yard average. We will use this information as we script our team periods in our practice schedule.

The down and distance breakdown gives the coach his opponent's tendencies in such critical situations as third and long, third and short, and fourth and short.

PRINTOUT 8-20

```
┌─────────────────────────────────────────────┐
│  TENDENCY FOR 1 DOWN AND 1 TO 10 YARDS        │
│               PASSING ZONES                   │
│  *******************************************  │
│                                               │
│                                               │
│            2          2         2             │
│                                               │
│   1        2          6         2        6    │
│                                               │
│            ------o o o o o------              │
│                         o                     │
│            1                    4             │
└─────────────────────────────────────────────┘
```

BY DOWN AND DISTANCE BY HASHMARKS
AND DIFFERENT FIELD ZONES

The last breakdown to be discussed is 6 = DOWN AND DISTANCE BREAKDOWN BY HASHMARKS AND DIFFERENT FIELD ZONES. We found through experience by evaluating our opponents after we have played them that we have gained the *least* amount of usable information from the most exact breakdown. We feel that this information becomes almost meaningless in its complexity. There are two exceptions to this rule where we have obtained excellent information:

1. When our opponent is coming out of his own end zone from the goal line to about their 15 yard line
2. When our opponent is going into our end zone from the five yard line and we are in a goal line defense

We have won some big games by using the breakdown in these two specific areas.

PRINTOUT 8-21

```
┌─────────────────────────────────────────────────┐
│  THE PASSING PLAYS                                │
│                                                   │
│  PASS/ATTEMPTS/COMPLETIONS/%ATTEM/TOT YD          │
│    3444.9   1            1           3      14    │
│                                                   │
│    3456.8   1            0           3      0     │
│                                                   │
│    3456.9   1            0           3      0     │
│                                                   │
│    3458.8   3            1           10     11    │
│                                                   │
│    3458.9   1            1           3      14    │
│                                                   │
│    3462.3   1            1           3      23    │
│                                                   │
│    3475.4   2            1           7      17    │
│                                                   │
│    4715     1            1           3      21    │
│                                                   │
│    4717.2   1            0           3      0     │
│                                                   │
│    4724.1   1            0           3      0     │
│                                                   │
│    4724.2   1            0           3      0     │
│                                                   │
│          ---MORE TO FOLLOW---                     │
│  READY                                            │
│  ?                                                │
│    4726.1   1            1           3      10    │
│                                                   │
│    5540     1            1           3      3     │
│                                                   │
│    5544.6   1            0           3      0     │
│                                                   │
│    5546.4   1            1           3      8     │
│                                                   │
│    5547.4   1            0           3      0     │
│                                                   │
│    5550     3            1           10     13    │
│                                                   │
│    5551.4   1            0           3      0     │
│                                                   │
│    5553     2            0           7      0     │
│                                                   │
│    5553.5   1            0           3      0     │
│                                                   │
│    5557.4   1            1           3      15    │
│                                                   │
│    5559     1            1           3      10    │
└─────────────────────────────────────────────────┘
```

PRINTOUT 8-22

```
┌─────────────────────────────────────────────────┐
│ TENDENCY FOR 1 DOWN AND 7 TO 10 YARDS             │
│              THE HOLE CHART                       │
│ 28 PASSES 40%                                     │
│                        HOLE #                     │
│        --9--7--5--3--1--0--2--4--6--8--           │
│ FREQ                                              │
│          9  2  2  3  2  3  3  3  3  12            │
│ PRCT                                              │
│         21  4  4  7  4  7  7  7  7  28            │
│ T.YD                                              │
│         26  2  2  5  4  2  25 20 8  7             │
│                                                   │
│                                                   │
│                                                   │
│               ----0   0   0   0   0----           │
│                              0                    │
│         ODD 42%                      EVEN57%      │
└─────────────────────────────────────────────────┘
```

PRINTOUT 8-23

PLAY	FREQ	PRCT	TOT.YDS	AVG.YDS
THE RUNNING PLAYS				
10	1	1	0	0
30.5	2	2	2	1
31.5	2	2	4	2
34	3	4	20	6
35	1	1	7	7
43	3	4	5	1
48	4	5	4	1
48.1	2	2	4	2
49	5	7	39	7
49.1	1	1	5	5
325	2	2	16	8

---MORE TO FOLLOW---

HIT A KEY WHEN YOU ARE READY

PRINTOUT 8-23 continued

342	1	1	0	0
461.8	2	2	7	3
465.5	1	1	1	1
471	1	1	-6	-6
471.8	3	4	11	3
472	1	1	-6	-6
483.8	1	1	15	15
554	2	2	-16	-8
555	2	2	-12	-6
3465.4	1	1	-5	-5
4828	1	1	6	6

A SUMMARY OF SAMPLE PLAYS

Table 8-1 summarizes the tendencies involving our sample plays. We have gained useful information on our four plays from a breakdown of our four charts. We now come to the next phase of our computerized scouting system—the preparation of a game plan. Every coach realizes that his advance information about an opponent must be used effectively in preparing his team for game time. In the next chapter we will put our knowledge to work as we prepare a game plan, implement a practice schedule, and put our players in as many anticipated situations in practice as possible. The personal computer makes the entire process more efficient.

TABLE 8-1

		PASSING GAME AND RUNNING GAME	
Play/ Total	**Hash**	**Formation**	**Down and Distance**
5550 (4)	Right (3 of 4)	I Pro Left Right End Split (4 of 4) Right Hash (3 of 4)	1st and long (3 of 4)
30.5 (7)	Right (4 of 7)	I Pro Left Right End Split (5 of 7) Right Hash (3 of 5)	2nd and long (3 of 7)
49 (10)	Left (6 of 10)	I Wing Left Right End Split (6 of 10) Left Hash (3 of 6) Middle (3 of 6)	1st and long (5 of 10)
471.8 (9)	Right (8 of 9)	I Pro Left Right End Split (6 of 9) Right Hash (5 of 6)	1st and long (3 of 9)

CHAPTER **9**

USING THE DATA

The following excerpt explaining the role, purpose, and process of the teacher is taken from *Teaching Physical Education in Secondary Schools* by Clyde Knapp and Patricia Leonhard. Its application to coaching and to using a personal computer is obvious.

> Teaching centers about the organization of learning experiences. Its purpose is to make learning more efficient. Teaching is the process of helping other individuals learn. A teacher (coach) plans the learning experiences of his students (players) in order that the learning process becomes as efficient as possible. He encourages learning by providing means of motivation which promote initial interest in learning and maintain a necessary level of interest until the student achieves the learning outcome. He also guides the learner through the learning experience, reducing to a minimum the amount of random or trial-and-error effort. He further serves as diagnostician, noting where progress toward goals has been misdirected; and he assists the learner to recognize acceptable progress and accomplishment of desired goals.

In this chapter we will use our computer data base and our defensive scheme as an example of how to organize a game plan and integrate the plan into a practice schedule to educate our players as efficiently as possible.

THE GAME PLAN FOLDER

Our defensive game plan folder is comprised of the following sections:

1. Defensive Scheme—listing of all defensive calls by front, stunt, coverage, blitz, rush, and drop.
2. Set Recognition—diagrams of all offensive formations used by our opponent, with corresponding defensive calls.

105

3. Running Game—diagrams of inside, outside, and trick running plays drawn against our base defense.

4. Passing Game—diagrams of play action, sprint out, and drop back passes drawn against our base coverages.

5. Goal Line—diagrams of goal line offense versus goal line defense.

6. Two-minute Offense—diagrams of two-minute offense versus our base defense.

7. Scout Team Script—listing of plays by sequence number, formation, description, hashmark, and down and distance tendencies.

8. Practice Schedule—game week breakdown for scheduled opponent.

9. Coaching Points—important points of emphasis by position.

10. Player's Report—general overview of opponent.

11. Computer Printout—strong tendencies underlined for ready reference.

The staff members responsible for each of these sections are as follows:

1. Defensive Scheme—Defensive Coordinator
2. Set Recognition—Linebacker Coach
3. Running Game—TNT Coach (inside),
   Defensive End Coach (outside, trick)
4. Passing Game—Secondary Coach
5. Goal Line—Linebacker Coach
6. Two-minute Offense—Secondary Coach
7. Scout Team Script—Defensive Coordinator,
   Scouting Coordinator
8. Practice Schedules—Defensive Coordinator
9. Coaching Points—Scouting Coordinator
10. Player's Report—Individual Scouting Teams
11. Computer Printouts—Scouting Coordinator

The biggest advantage to using a computerized scouting system is that it frees us from the time-consuming, tedious task of shuffling through scouting materials. This allows us to use our time organizing a game plan, integrating that plan into our practice schedule, and having all of it accomplished when we step onto the practice field to begin a new week. This is as organized for practice, as efficient with available time, and as well-versed on an opponent as we can be. This will have a great influence on the players who will be the ones actually executing this game plan at the end of the week. There will be few if any situations to be faced during a game that haven't been faced on the practice field and we can expect an improvement in team performance.

A DEFENSIVE SCHEME

All defensive calls that we anticipate using are recorded on a card with specific entries for these six categories:

TABLE 9-1

A DEFENSIVE SCHEME

Front	Stunt	Coverage	Blitz	Rush	Drop
Eagle		Cover 1		5	6
		2 Combo		5	6
		3 Squat		5	6
Eagle G		Cover 1		5	6
		2 Combo		5	6
		3 Squat		5	6
Over		Cover 1		5	6
		2 Combo		5	6
		3 Squat		5	6
Eagle G Special		3 Special		5	6
Split Pro		Cover 1		4	7
		2 Combo		4	7
		3 Squat		4	7
		Cover 6		4	7
Slide		Cover 4		4	7
	Sam Plug	Cover 4		5	6
	Mike Plug	Cover 4		5	6
	Ed Plug	Cover 4		5	6
50		Cover 6 Special		3	8
40		Cover 5		4	7
Hog		Man		6	5
	Guts	Man	Safety Hammer	7	4
Hog Slide		Man		6	5

1. Front—alignment and responsibilities of down linemen, stand up ends, and linebackers.
2. Stunt—predetermined movement of the front.
3. Coverage—alignment and responsibilities of the secondary.
4. Blitz—predetermined movement of a defensive back.
5. Rush—number of personnel attacking the quarterback on pass
6. Drop—number of personnel defending receivers on pass.

SET RECOGNITION

All offensive formations used by our opponent are drawn with the corresponding defensive calls listed for each (Diagrams 9-1 through 9-6). These formations are taken from our formation coding key (Chapter 5, Diagrams 5-3 through 5-8). They are listed starting with the most used formation and ending with the least used or special situation formations. Goal line formations or two-minute offense formations are examples of special situation formations.

Eagle	Slide
Eagle G	50
Over	40
Split Pro	Hog

DIAGRAM 9-1

Eagle	Slide
Eagle G	50
Over	40
Split Pro	Hog

DIAGRAM 9-2

Eagle	50
Eagle G	40
Over	Hog
Slide	

DIAGRAM 9-3

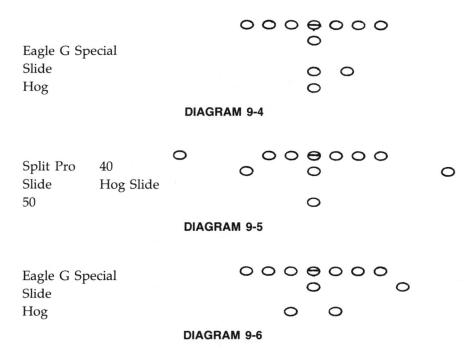

Eagle G Special
Slide
Hog

DIAGRAM 9-4

Split Pro   40
Slide   Hog Slide
50

DIAGRAM 9-5

Eagle G Special
Slide
Hog

DIAGRAM 9-6

THE RUNNING GAME

All inside, outside, and trick running plays are drawn versus our base defense. We have included the following three running plays, previously charted in Chapter 4 on our offensive scouting form, as examples (Diagrams 9-7 through 9-9):

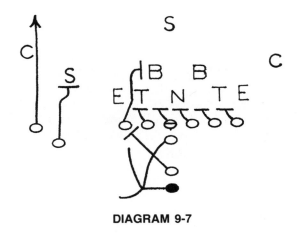

DIAGRAM 9-7

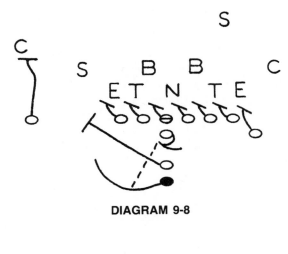

DIAGRAM 9-8

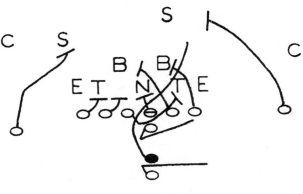

DIAGRAM 9-9

THE PASSING GAME

All play action, sprint out, and drop back passing plays are drawn versus our base coverage. The following three passing plays (Diagrams 9-10 through 9-12) are offered as examples. Notice that the drop back pass was charted in Chapter 4 on our offensive scouting form:

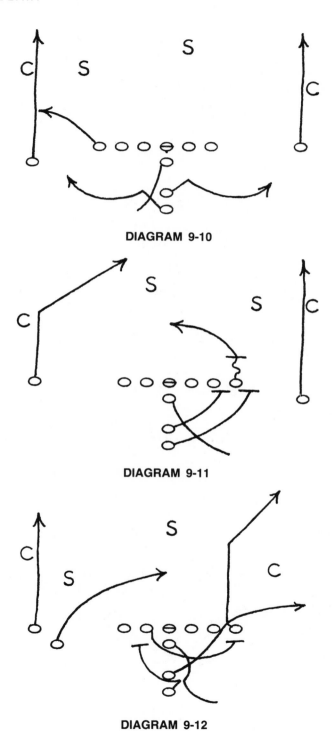

DIAGRAM 9-10

DIAGRAM 9-11

DIAGRAM 9-12

GOAL LINE

All goal line runs and passes are drawn versus our goal line defense. We have included these three plays as examples (Diagrams 9-13 through 9-15):

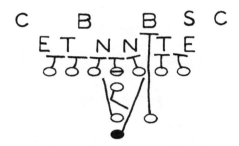

DIAGRAM 9-13

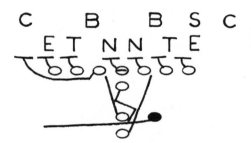

DIAGRAM 9-14

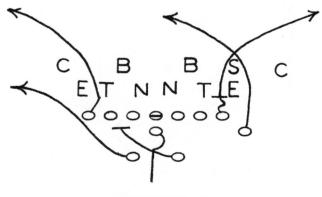

DIAGRAM 9-15

TWO-MINUTE OFFENSE

All two-minute offense plays are drawn versus our base defense. We present the following three plays as examples (Diagrams 9-16 through 9-18):

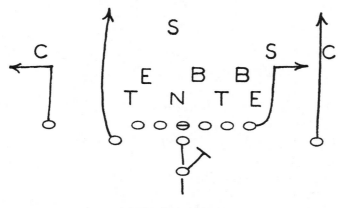

DIAGRAM 9-16

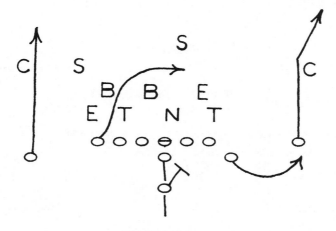

DIAGRAM 9-17

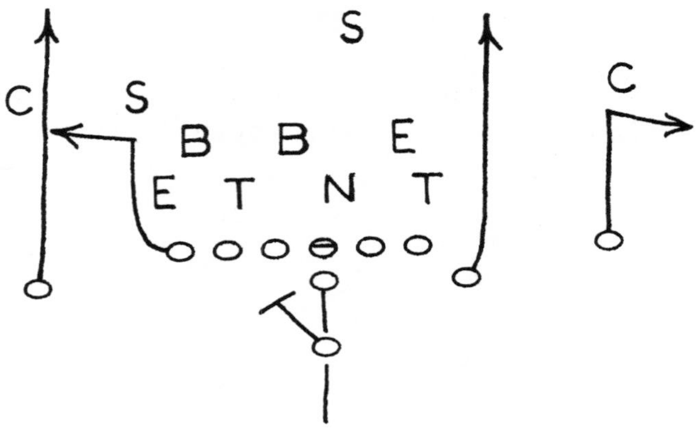

DIAGRAM 9-18

THE SCOUT TEAM SCRIPT

The scout team script lists all plays by sequence number, formation, description, hashmark, and down and distance tendency. It is used by all our team coaches as a reference during team periods on our practice schedule. The sequence number may be changed during the practice week depending on what we want to emphasize. An abbreviated example is presented in Table 9-2.

TABLE 9-2

	THE SCOUT TEAM SCRIPT				
Sequence	Formation	Description	Hash	Down/ Distance	Defense
1	IProL RES	5550	R	1 L	Slide Cover 4
2	IProL RES	471.8	R	1 L	Over 2 Combo
3	IWingL RES	49	L	1 L	Eagle G 2 Combo
4	IProL RES	30.5	R	2 L	Eagle Cover 1

THE PRACTICE SCHEDULES

We divide our Monday, Tuesday, and Wednesday schedules (Schedules 9-1 through 9-3) into five-minute blocks of time. Our Thursday practice schedule (Schedule 9-4) is a team substitution drill. You will notice two trends that are part of these schedules:

SCHEDULE 9-1

Monday Practice Schedule					
2:00	1	Stretch			
	2				
2:10	3	Offense			
	4				
	5				
	6				
	7				
	8				
	9				
	10				
	11				
	12				
	13				
	14				
	15				
	16				
	17				
3:25	18	Break			
3:30	19	Defense—Drills and Techniques			
	20	TNT	E	B	Secondary
	21				
	22				
	23				
	24				
4:00	25	Inside Runs	Outside Runs		
	26				
	27				
4:15	28	Front 5 Rush/Drop	Pass Coverage		
	29				
	30				
4:30	31	Team Defense			
	32				
	33				
4:45	34	Kicking Game			
	35				
	36				
5:00	37	End of Practice			

SCHEDULE 9-2

Tuesday Practice Schedule					
2:00	1	Stretch			
	2				
2:10	3	Offense			
	4				
	5				
	6				
	7				
	8				
	9				
	10				
	11				
	12				
	13				
	14				
	15				
	16				
	17				
3:25	18	Break			
3:30	19	Defense—Drills and Techniques			
	20	TNT	E	B	Secondary
	21				
	22	Inside Runs	Outside Runs		
	23				
	24				
	25	Front 5 RushDrop	Pass Coverage		
	26				
	27				
	28	Team Defense			
	29				
	30				
	31				
	32				
	33	Goalline			
4:45	34	Kicking Game			
	35				
	36				
5:00	37	End of Practice			

SCHEDULE 9-3

Wednesday Practice Schedule					
2:00	1	Stretch			
	2				
2:10	3	Offense			
	4				
	5				
	6				
	7				
	8				
	9				
	10				
2:50	11	Defense—Drills and Techniques			
	12	TNT	E	B	Secondary
	13	Inside Runs	Outside Runs		
	14				
	15				
	16	Front 5 Rush/Drop	Pass Coverage		
	17				
	18				
3:30	19	Break			
3:35	20	Team Offense	Team Defense		
	21	vs.	vs.		
	22	Reserves	J.V.		
	23				
	24				
	25				
4:05	26		Goalline		
	27				
4:15	28	Kicking Game			
	29				
	30				
4:30	31	End of Practice			

SCHEDULE 9-4

Thursday Practice Schedule

1. We elect to receive.
2. Receive kickoff.
   First offense run play and score.
3. Kick extra point.
4. Kickoff team.
   First defense, hold them on third down.
5. Punt return team.
   Second offense run play, get stopped.
6. Punt team.
   Second defense, force safety.
7. Kickoff receiving team, receive kick after safety.
   First offense, run play and get stopped.
8. Punt to inside ten, coffin corner or hang it up.
   Punt team stay on field and turn around.
9. Tight punt.
10. Take a safety.
11. Kickoff after a safety.

1. We spend progressively *less* total practice time *on the field* as we move from the beginning of the week toward game day. This is from a maximum of three hours on Monday to less than an hour on Thursday for a Friday night game.
2. We spend progressively *more* defensive practice time *in team situations* as we move from the beginning of the week toward game day. This is from a minimum of 15 minutes on Monday to a maximum of 40 minutes on Wednesday. Thursday is devoted entirely to a team substitution drill.

We feel this is necessary for three reasons:

1. More individual instruction is required early in the week, which dictates a longer practice time.
2. Placing the player in more game-type situations is required later in the week, which dictates more team periods.
3. The psychological and physical effects of shorter practices as the week progresses is a motivational factor in the preparation of the players for the game.

COACHING POINTS

The important coaching points to be emphasized are listed by position. This is designed as a quick reference for our position coaches as they plan the use of individual technique periods (Table 9-3).

TABLE 9-3

COACHING POINTS

Position	Call	Coaching Points
TNT		Trap
		Double
	Split Pro	Contain
	Slide	Contain
	50	Contain
E		Hook
		F block
	Split Pro	Ed-C gap, near back, hook to curl
	Slide	Ed-B gap, near back, curl
	50	Regular-near back, twist
		Ed-near back, twist
B		Isolation
	Slide	Sam-C gap, near back, hook to curl
		Mike-A gap, draw, middle hook
	50	Wall
	40	Near back
Secondary		Crack
		Lead
		Motion

THE PLAYER'S REPORT

A general overview of our opponent is given to each of our players. It includes:

1. Offensive Personnel
2. Defensive Personnel

3. Favorite Formations
4. Favorite Running Plays
5. Favorite Passing Plays
6. Base Defense and Favorite Change-Ups
7. Goal Line Defense
8. Kicking Game Trick Plays

All other information on our opponent will be covered on the practice field.

COMPUTER PRINTOUTS

We keep our computer printouts on file by breakdown with strong tendencies underlined in red for ready reference. We will refer to them during the practice week, before the game, during the game, and at halftime as the need arises.

All sections of our game plan folder are duplicated and distributed to our coaches. The master copy of each of the first nine sections is laminated by our audio-visual department on Monday morning as a precaution in case of inclement weather.

In this chapter we have discussed how our computer data base is used to organize a game plan and to integrate the plan into our practice schedule using our defensive scheme as an example. We feel that the personal computer frees our coaches from having to spend a lot of time shuffling through scouting materials. The time gained can now be spent organizing a game plan and integrating that plan into a practice schedule. All of this can now be accomplished before our staff takes the field on Monday afternoon.

CHAPTER **10**

ORGANIZING FOR GAME DAY

We have now come to the final phase in the use of a computerized scouting system. In this chapter we will discuss three important areas:

1. Sideline and Press Box Organization
2. Halftime Procedures
3. Postgame Analysis

We will relate our comments to our defensive staff as we discuss the forms and charts that we use. Finally, we will discuss our self-scouting procedures that have been of great value to our system. The size of your football coaching staff will determine how much of your game-day system you may be able to implement; but our system would be incomplete without a discussion of what takes place during and after a game.

SIDELINE AND PRESS BOX

During a game we have four coaches who work specifically with the defense. The arrangement of these coaches is at the discretion of the defensive coordinator who may prefer to be on the sideline or in the pressbox. We have found that the best results are achieved with one defensive coach on the sideline and the other three defensive coaches in the press box. Their responsibilities are listed in Table 10-1.

We will also utilize one of the two scouts as a defensive spotter in the press box. His major responsibility is to watch for substitutions or new formations and plays being used by our opponent, or any unexpected tendencies that may emerge during the game. Considering the number of staff members that we have available and the feedback that we desire, these organizational procedures produce the best results.

TABLE 10-1

STAFF RESPONSIBILITIES DURING GAME		
Coach	**Location**	**Responsibilities**
1	Sideline	Remain in constant radio or telephone communication with Coach 2.
		Give all defensive calls to the defensive captain by prearranged hand signals, and to the press box by radio or telephone if necessary.
		Make all defensive substitutions.
		Relate all coaching points to the defensive players at a predesignated location after each change of possession.
2	Press Box	Remain in constant radio or telephone communication with Coach 1.
		Relate all pertinent information to the sideline such as hashmark, yardline, down and distance, formation, play, result, and offensive substitutions.
		Maintain ready access to all material in the game plan folder.
		Relay tendency changes to the field.
		Act as a defensive liaison between the sideline and the press box.
		Watch your defensive personnel.
3	Press Box	Keep lateral field position chart by down and distance (Chart 10-1).
		Keep strength tendency chart by down and distance (Chart 10-2).
		Relay pertinent information to Coach 2.
		Watch your defensive personnel.
4	Press Box	Keep defensive-offensive calls chart by listening to Coach 2 (Chart 10-3).
		Relay pertinent information to Coach 2.
		Watch your defensive personnel.

CHART 10-1

	Run Wideside	Pass Wideside	Middle	Run Shortside	Pass Shortside
LATERAL FIELD POSITION BY DOWN AND DISTANCE					
1					
2					
3					
4					
5					
6					
7					
8					
9					
10					
11					
12					
13					
14					
15					
16					
17					
18					
19					
20					
21					
22					
23					
24					
25					
26					

CHART 10-2

	Run Strength	Pass Strength	Middle	Run Weakside	Pass Weakside
STRENGTH TENDENCIES BY DOWN AND DISTANCE					
1					
2					
3					
4					
5					
6					
7					
8					
9					
10					
11					
12					
13					
14					
15					
16					
17					
18					
19					
20					
21					
22					
23					
24					
25					
26					
27					
28					
29					
30					
31					
32					
33					
34					

CHART 10-3

NO.	D & D	HASH	DEFENSE		OFFENSE		RESULT	COMMENTS
			CALL	CHECK	SET	PLAY		

HALF TIME

Our defensive half time procedure is divided into three segments for the time available:

1. Defensive staff meeting
2. Coaches-players meetings by position
3. Defensive team meeting

The defensive staff will meet as soon as all coaches reach the locker room from the press box or sideline. At this time any particular problems or change in tendencies that have occurred will be discussed and an appropriate solution determined within our defensive game plan and scheme. This is a relaxation time for the players.

Each position coach will then meet with the players for whom he is responsible. It is important that this be a two-way discussion so that the position coach and all the players have a better understanding of what is really happening on the field, and so that the individual player has an awareness of what is happening to him personally.

Then the entire defensive staff and defensive unit will meet for an overview presented by the defensive coordinator. Other position coaches may make comments as time permits. This final meeting should end with a few appropriate remarks which will give the team an emotional lift before going out for the second half.

POSTGAME ANALYSIS

We use five different forms or charts in our postgame analysis:

1. Offensive Statistics
2. Field Position Chart
3. Defensive Goals Chart
4. Defensive-Offensive Calls Form
5. Offensive Scouting Form

The first three—offensive statistics, field position chart, and goals chart—are completed in the coach's office immediately after the game. The last two—defensive-offensive calls chart and offensive scouting forms—are completed after we have received the processed game film from our photographer.

The offensive statistics (Printouts 10-1 through 10-3) are used to chart the offensive possessions, the running game, the passing game, and the team statistics of our opponent. This information is taken from the defensive-offensive calls chart which was kept by Coach 4 in the press box during the game.

The field position chart (Chart 10-4) is a visual representation of our opponent's possessions. This information is taken from the offensive statistics.

The defensive goal chart (Chart 10-5) is posted in our locker room and is used as a motivational device for our players. This information is also taken from the offensive statistics.

The comments column of the defensive-offensive calls chart (Chart 10-3) is used to record individual coaching points on our defensive personnel during postgame film breakdown. These coaching

OFF POS	START	PLAYS	DEF PENA	1ST DOWNS	3D CONVER	STOP	RESULT
1	-16	3	5	0	0	-24	PUNT
2	-29	6	0	1	1	-39	PUNT
3	44	4	0	1	0	4	F.G.
4	38	7	0	2	0	8	F.G.
5	-20	3	0	0	0	-27	PUNT
6	-27	1	0	0	0	-27	HALF
7	-30	3.	0	0	0	-39	PUNT
8	-38	5	0	2	1	0	T.D.
9	-34	3	0	0	0	-41	PUNT
10	-33	8	0	2	1	43	PUNT
11	42	8	0	3	2	0	T.D.
TOTALS		51	5	11	5		

127

RUNNING GAME

1ST Q	2ND Q	3RD Q	4TH Q
3	1	2	12
0	8	2	3
6	0	1	0
2	7	6	-9
1	1	2	1
	3	5	-4
	6	0	4
	0		1
	3		2
	4		11
	0		2
			1
			1
12	33	18	25

PASSING GAME

1ST Q	2ND Q	3RD Q	4TH Q
0	32	5	0
0	9	0	21
6	11	11	16
0	0	42	
		3	
6	52	61	37

PRINTOUT 10-3

RUSHES	YARDS	FUMBLES	AVERAGE	COMP	ATTEMPT	INTERCEP	YARDS
36	88	0/2	2.4444444	10	16	0	156

AVERAGE

15.6

TOTAL YARD

244

CHART 10-4

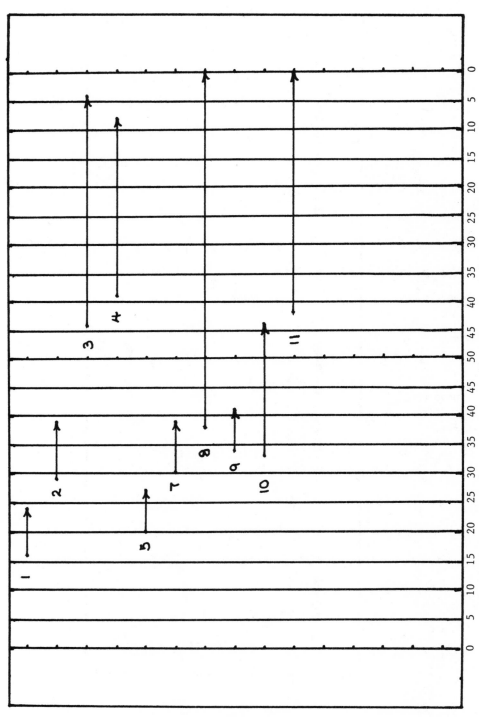

130

CHART 10-5

DEFENSIVE GOALS PER GAME										
Do not let them score from inside our 20										
Not more than 11 plays in a possession										
Never allow our goalline defense to give up a TD										
No Gifts: Allow no runs of more than 20 yards										
No Gifts: Never be beaten by a long pass for a touch-down										
Sudden Change: Get one interception for every 13 passes										
Sudden Change: Cause a minimum of 3 turnovers by being physical										
Allow no more than 3 third down conversions										
Five Times "Three-and-Off"										
Hold opponent to less than 230 yards total offense										
No penalties that keep a drive alive										
Defensive Shutout										
Execute Defense called in the huddle and any neces-sary checks										

1st game	6th game
2nd game	7th game
3rd game	8th game
4th game	9th game
5th game	10th game

points are the basis for comments made by the coaches during our defensive film sessions with the players and are itemized by position and posted in our locker room.

The offensive scouting form (Form 10-1) is used to analyze our opponent's tendencies using a personal computer as described earlier in this book. This has proved to be an excellent method of self-analysis for our coaches as we are continually attempting to evaluate our individual coaching decisions within the total system. This completes the circle of evaluation before, during, and after a ball game.

In this chapter we have given an overview of our game day organization. We feel that the press box-to-sideline, half time, and postgame procedures that we use complement our entire computerized scouting system. Of course, we are always looking for ways to best utilize our time, our players, and ourselves.

A WORD TO THE SCOUTS

We would be remiss if we did not recognize the most important link in our computerized scouting chain—the scouts themselves. We feel that it is extremely important to acknowledge their work, especially at the end of the season. A simple thank you for a job well-done is appropriate. Here is a sample letter which we have sent to all of our scouts in the past to show appreciation of their contribution to our program:

TO: Varsity Scouts

FROM: Scouting Coordinator

Now that our varsity football season has been completed and we have begun our off-season program, I would like to thank our varsity scouts for the fine job done during the past season. The success we achieved can be directly attributed to the high quality of information brought back on our opponents. Thank you for the hours spent preparing for your assignments, scouting the teams, compiling the data, and assisting us in the press box. Your behind the scenes contribution to our program is recognized and appreciated.

Thanks again,

Alan B. Hatfield
Scouting Coordinator

FORM 10-1

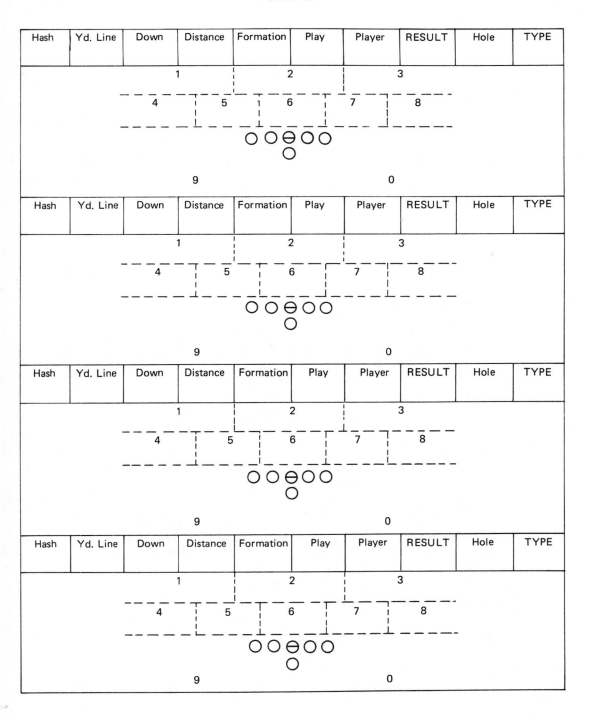

Hash	Yd. Line	Down	Distance	Formation	Play	Player	RESULT	Hole	TYPE

1   2   3
4   5   6   7   8
9   0

Hash	Yd. Line	Down	Distance	Formation	Play	Player	RESULT	Hole	TYPE

1   2   3
4   5   6   7   8
9   0

Hash	Yd. Line	Down	Distance	Formation	Play	Player	RESULT	Hole	TYPE

1   2   3
4   5   6   7   8
9   0

Hash	Yd. Line	Down	Distance	Formation	Play	Player	RESULT	Hole	TYPE

1   2   3
4   5   6   7   8
9   0

CHAPTER 11

CHOOSING YOUR SOFTWARE

We began this book with a discussion of hardware; we will end it with a discussion of software. When you have decided that a computerized scouting system is for you, choose your software *first* and then get your hardware. We have waited to present a discussion of software as our last topic because by now you are computer-literate enough to take your first step toward setting up a computerized scouting system of your own.

LANGUAGES AND PROGRAMS

Because most humans think best in terms of words, phrases, and sentences, while computers manipulate numbers, a mutually acceptable language must be used in order for humans and computers to communicate. Presently, the most popular computer language is called BASIC (Beginner's All-Purpose Symbolic Instruction Code). BASIC is flexible, versatile, and relies on such familiar English words as *data, go to, print,* and *read.* BASIC allows nonmathematicians to use computers and even write specialized programs.

A program is nothing more than an explicit, step-by-step sequence of instructions that tell the computer *exactly* what you want it to do. Software is the general name for all computer programs. Without this software a computer is as worthless as a phonograph without a record, but when coupled with the right software the computer becomes a powerful tool for manipulating information.

Even though you may never write your own program, it is important that you understand the different types of languages and the different types of software that are working for you in a desk-top computer. There are three levels of language at work in the computer. The most fundamental is called machine language; the next is called assembly language; and the last is called high-level language. The machine language is determined by the particular microprocessor (see Chapter 1) that is used in your personal computer. It is the lowest level language, or the most fundamental, because it is made up of bytes that tell the electronic components of the computer what to do. This is the only language that the microprocessor can use or directly understand, but it is completely incomprehensible to anyone but a mathematician.

The next is called assembly language. It uses a special program called an assembler which allows the user to write programs where the individual machine language instructions are written in symbolic form for easier programming. The assembler acts as a translator to convert assembly language into machine language. The high-level language is the easiest of the three to use. Therefore, this is the language that most programmers learn. An interpreter or compiler converts high-level language into assembly language. Some of the common high-level languages have been listed in Table 11-1. Most football scouting programs for personal computers are written in BASIC, which is actually a family of very similar languages. Each computer company uses its own variation or dialect of BASIC. Some of the newer football scouting programs are being written in Pascal which utilizes the maximum potential of your computer to process data quickly. Usually, languages that are easier to use are, however, slower to operate.

Just as there are different levels of language at work inside the computer, there are also different types of software that utilize those languages in order for your computer to operate efficiently. The operating systems programs are sets of instructions written in machine language that let you use all the pieces of your computer (disk drive, monitor, printer) as an integrated computer system. There are also utility programs which accomplish specific jobs such as diagnostic checks of your equipment; and there are routine programs which are stored in ROM and perform other useful tasks. Such programs stored in ROM are called firmware because they can be executed at any time but cannot be modified or erased from memory. When you purchase your hardware make sure that it is CP/M compatible or can be made so by the addition of an adaptor card. CP/M stands for Control Program for Microcomputers which means that it is not written for a particular computer but can be used by many brands. This is the closest the industry has come to standardization to date. The last type of program

TABLE 11-1

HIGH-LEVEL LANGUAGES		
Language	**Origin of the Name**	**Application Example**
Ada	Ada Augusta, Countess of Lovelace (1816–1852), who is reputed to have been "the world's first programmer."	robot intelligence
ALGOL	ALGOrithm Language	general purpose
APL	A Programming Language	business statistics
BASIC	Beginner's All-Purpose Symbolic Instruction Code	beginning programming
C	Developed as part of a series, the previous units were designated A and B.	portable, systems programming
COBOL	COmmon Business-Oriented Language	business and commercial data processing
FORTH	shortened form of FOURTH generation of computers	flexible, systems programming, making the best use of a computer's speed and memory
FORTRAN	FORmula TRANslator	mathematics, engineering, and science
LISP	LISt Processor	research in artificial intelligence
Logo	—	instructional language for children
Modula-2	programs consist of independent modules	systems programming
Pascal	17th century French mathematician	business applications
Pilot	serving as a guiding device	computer aided instruction
PL/I	—	business, science
PROLOG	PROgramming in LOGic	artificial intelligence and fifth generation computers
Savvy	—	pattern-recognition
Small talk	—	robot intelligence

SPEED OF OPERATION (fastest to slowest)

———————————▶——————————▶—————————▶

machine language   assembly language   BASIC, etc.

EASE OF PROGRAMMING (easiest to hardest)

———————————▶——————————▶—————————▶

BASIC, etc.   assembly language   machine language

DIAGRAM 11-1

is called an applications program. As the name implies, these sets of instructions are written for specific applications—like breaking down tendencies in a football scouting report. This brief overview of languages and programs has, we hope, given you a better idea of the many things going on inside your computer as it operates.

IMPORTANT CONSIDERATIONS

When you are selecting the specific football scouting program to meet your needs within your budget, there are several important considerations to keep in mind. When writing for information, ask about the following:

1. Specifically, how is the data collected at the game site? What forms are used?
2. How must I compile the data for input into the computer? How is the actual input accomplished? Do I use DATA statements or is it menu-driven?
3. How is the data output after processing? Are sample printouts available?
4. How flexible is the football terminology and/or numbering system? May I use my own terminology or am I locked into a set of predetermined terminology?
5. What are the specific limitations as to the number of offensive formations, offensive players, and number of games that may be *input* and *processed* at one time?

6. How versatile is the program as far as including various pass routes and various blocking schemes when analyzing my opponent's passing game and running game?
7. Does the program contain a self-check system to alert me as to input errors?
8. Can you supply a list of references—schools that are now using your software? Do you have an emergency or hot line number that may be used should problems arise?

WHAT IS AVAILABLE NOW

Listed here are 32 suppliers and 38 programs presented in alphabetical order. Included are the name of the program, business address and phone number of the company that sells it, the necessary hardware for its operation, price of the software, and some personal comments. Any questions concerning the programs should be directed to the supplier.

NAME:	All American Scouting
ADDRESS:	Wes Pyfer 1920 Sandy Lane Irving, Texas 75060
PHONE:	(214) 399-8094
HARDWARE:	Apple II, II+, //e, or III (48K) Single disk drive 80 column printer
SOFTWARE:	$625

NAME:	Blitz
ADDRESS:	Robert R. Cornelison Route 2, Box 2684 Sunnyside, Washington 98944
PHONE:	(509) 965-4788
HARDWARE:	Apple II, II+, or //e Radio Shack TRS-80 Models I, III, or 4
SOFTWARE:	$395

NAME: Champs #26-2703

ADDRESS: Radio Shack Education Division
                 Dept. 83-1-496
                 300 One Tandy Center
                 Fort Worth, Texas 76102

PHONE: (817) 390-3832

HARDWARE: TRS-80 Models I and II (48K)
                 Radio Shack 132 column printer

SOFTWARE: $149.95

COMMENTS: An excellent scouting manual is included

NAME: Champs/O

ADDRESS: Bruce Turkiewicz
                 P. O. Box 1944
                 Spring, Texas 77383

PHONE: (713) 353-1777

HARDWARE: TRS-80 Model III or IV (48K, 132 column printer)
                 Apple II, II+, //e, or //c (48K, 132 column printer or
                 80 column printer in compressed mode)

SOFTWARE: $299

COMMENTS: This is an enhanced version of the original. Selective
                 printouts are available. A defensive package,
                 Champs/D, may also be purchased for $299 or both
                 offense and defense for $549.

NAME: Compu-Scout

ADDRESS: 4714 Lasheart Drive
                 La Canada - Flintridge, California 91011

PHONE: (213) 790-3018

HARDWARE: Apple II and //e
                 Two disk drives
                 Joystick
                 132 column printer

SOFTWARE: $495 to $1249

COMMENTS: Compu-Scout's experience with mainframe scouting
               programs is evident in the quality of their personal
               computer edition. This program is written in Pascal. It
               is menu-driven with entries being made by using a
               joystick. You may use 13 different run descriptions,
               15 different pass descriptions, and 17 different pass
               route descriptions. It is an excellent system for
               scouting directly off a game film. A defensive package
               is also available.

NAME: Computer Athletics

ADDRESS: Max Boydston Sales Co.
               1102 South Elm
               Sherman, Texas 75090

PHONE: (214) 892-3062

HARDWARE: Apple II, II Plus, and //e
               Commodore Pet 4032 and 80
               TRS-80 Model I, III, and 4

SOFTWARE: $300

COMMENTS: We have used an early version of this program since
               1978. It can process about 200 plays and 99
               formations. Newer versions are even more user
               friendly than the original.

NAME: Computer Programs Unlimited

ADDRESS: Sports Division
               5614 Innsbruck
               Bellaire, Texas 77401

PHONE: (713) 665-6007

HARDWARE: Apple II Plus and //e
               Epson MX-80 printer

SOFTWARE: $250

COMMENTS: This program is written in machine language (binary)
               which means it runs extremely fast. You can use 16
               entries to process a maximum of 90 plays with up to

70 runs or up to 45 passes in the total. Forty different run descriptions, 30 different formation descriptions, and 20 different pass route descriptions are possible. This is an excellent program for single game analysis when you want your printout as fast as possible.

NAME:	Eagle Computer System
ADDRESS:	J. B. Padgett Box 1484 Euless, Texas 76039
PHONE:	(817) 267-1698
HARDWARE:	Apple II+, //e (48K) Single disk drive
SOFTWARE:	$725
COMMENTS:	15 menu-driven entries are made for a maximum of 300 plays and 50 formations. Unique data checking, edit, and search features are included with 22 total reports.

NAME:	Easy-Scout
ADDRESS:	Nick Interdonato Comp-U-Sports, Inc. P. O. Box 1340 Frederick, Maryland 21701
PHONE:	(301) 663-3257
HARDWARE:	Apple //c
SOFTWARE:	$100
COMMENTS:	A multiple game version will allow up to 5 games to be combined to produce a composite report. A quarterly "Coaching with Computers" newsletter is sent to registered users.

NAME:	Football Scout
ADDRESS:	W. C. Royle Company 309 Laurel Lufkin, Texas 75901

PHONE: TX 1-800-392-3701
                (713) 634-4468

HARDWARE: Apple
                Commodore
                Intertec
                Radio Shack

SOFTWARE: $985

NAME: Football Scout

ADDRESS: Midwest Software
                Box 214
                Farmington, Michigan 48024

PHONE: (313) 477-0897

HARDWARE: Apple II+ or //e (32K)
                Commodore 64
                Pet (32K)

SOFTWARE: $79.95, Demo disk $5

COMMENTS: This program allows 50 plays per game for six games
                to be input. You may define five field zones, down
                and distance values, and formations.

NAME: Football Scout

ADDRESS: Athletic Computer Programs
                P. O. Box 9146
                College Station, Texas 77840

PHONE: (409) 696-2921

HARDWARE: Radio Shack TRS-80 Models III and 4

SOFTWARE: $99.95

COMMENTS: Both offensive and defensive scouting programs are
                available.

NAME: Football Scouting   ADDRESS: George King
                                                      Big G Software
                                                      Route 2, Box 111
                                                      Alleyton, Texas 78935

PHONE: (409) 732-3904

HARDWARE: TRS-80

SOFTWARE: $49.95

NAME: Football Scouting System

ADDRESS: Larry Hilsabeck
              Computer Products
              286 E. Mission Road
              Corona, California 91720

HARDWARE: Apple II
              TRS-80

SOFTWARE: $40–$60

NAME: Gamestat

ADDRESS: Don Knezek
              Micros Illuminated
              Box 745
              Olney, Texas 76374

PHONE: (817) 725-5308

HARDWARE: Apple II Plus, //e, and III
              40 column printer
              Radio Shack

SOFTWARE: $90

COMMENTS: This program is designed to be used during games to
              keep track of your opponent's tendencies while you
              play them. It is an excellent source for half-time
              statistics for analysis.

NAME: Grant Teaff Computer Scouting

ADDRESS: TAFCO Inc.
              P. O. Box 2126
              Waco, Texas 76706

PHONE: (817) 754-4648

HARDWARE: Texas Instruments TI-99/4A

SOFTWARE: $200

COMMENTS: This program will process up to four games at one time. Seventy-five different formation descriptions, 99 different play descriptions, 20 different pass descriptions, and ten different pass route descriptions are possible. Sixteen entries are made per play. Now that Texas Instruments is no longer in the personal computer business, its hardware may be available at bargain prices and this could be an excellent way to begin a computerized scouting system very inexpensively. The purchaser will likely sacrifice the support of the manufacturer, however.

NAME: Grid Scout

ADDRESS: Microscout
             2161 Mills Avenue
             Menlo Park, California 94025

PHONE: (415) 854-4718

HARDWARE: Apple II, II Plus, and //e (48K)
             TRS-80 Model III (48K)
             2 disk drives
             132 column printer

SOFTWARE: $249.95

COMMENTS: This program can process 12 games at one time. A defensive version can process 14 games.

NAME: M-SCOUT

ADDRESS: Micro-sher Inc.
             P. O. Box 13688
             Arlington, Texas 76013

PHONE: (817) 457-7762

HARDWARE: Apple //e
             Single disk drive
             Epson or Centronics printer

SOFTWARE: $400

NAME: Masterscout

ADDRESS: Computer Recovery Inc.
                 Route 4
                 Box 860
                 Alvarado, Texas 76009

PHONE: (817) 783-2208

HARDWARE: Apple II, II Plus, and //e

NAME: P.A.S.S. Computer Scouting

ADDRESS: Superior Athletic Systems
                 P. O. Box 1082
                 Grapevine, Texas 76051

PHONE: (817) 481-4838

HARDWARE: Apple II Plus and //e
                 80 column printer

SOFTWARE: $600 to $850

COMMENTS: This program is menu-driven with alphanumeric
                 input. Three hundred plays (five games) may be
                 processed at one time from nine games stored.
                 Twenty-three entries are made per play with up to
                 eight characters for some entries. Its printouts are
                 very well formatted.

NAME: Quick Scout

ADDRESS: Software Associates of North East
                 P. O. Box 70
                 North East, Pennsylvania 16428

PHONE: (814) 725-9279
                 (814) 725-5308

HARDWARE: Apple (48K)
                 80 column printer

SOFTWARE: $130

COMMENTS: A statistics program with 14 categories is also
                 available.

NAME: Quickstat

ADDRESS: Don Knezek
                 Micros Illuminated
                 Box 745
                 Olney, Texas 76374

PHONE: (817) 873-4550

HARDWARE: Apple II (48K)
                 Two disk drives recommended
                 80 column printer

SOFTWARE: $155

COMMENTS: 19 entries per play may be used. 20 games may be
                 analyzed. 60 play names, formations, and ball
                 handlers are allowed. Dstat for defensive scouting is
                 also available.

NAME: RVM

ADDRESS: Rick Vansickle
                 P. O. Box 341
                 Aztec, New Mexico 87410

PHONE: (505) 334-6445

HARDWARE: Apple

NAME: Scoutmaster Football

ADDRESS: 1761 6th Street
                 Los Asos, California 93402

PHONE: (805) 528-4646

HARDWARE: Apple II, II Plus, and //e

SOFTWARE: $250

NAME: Scoutronics

ADDRESS: Bob Campbell
                 5475 Salt Box Lane
                 Clay, New York 13401

PHONE: (315) 699-4689

HARDWARE: Apple, Franklin

NAME: Soft-Mix Enterprises

ADDRESS: Ray Mixell
                 737 N. Governer Road
                 Valparaiso, Indiana 46383

PHONE: (219) 759-3667

HARDWARE: Apple, Commodore Pet

NAME: Stat-Man

ADDRESS: Forrest Bone
                 ARC Computer Services
                 1870 Southfield
                 Dearborn, Michigan 48125

PHONE: (313) 593-4495

HARDWARE: Apple
                 TRS-80

NAME: Super Scout

ADDRESS: Art Klein
                 Computerized Football Aids
                 P. O. Box 114
                 Arlington Heights, Illinois 60006

PHONE: (312) 577-7816

HARDWARE: Apple II
                 Commodore Pet, 64
                 TRS-80

SOFTWARE: $79.95

NAME: Super Scout

ADDRESS: 3213 S. Glenbrook Drive
                 Garland, Texas 75041

PHONE: (214) 278-4211 and 271-5733

HARDWARE: Apple II
             KayPro
             TRS-80
             80 column printer

SOFTWARE: $550

COMMENTS: This program uses 13 entries per play to process up
             to 300 plays. Sixteen formations, pass, and run
             descriptions are possible with up to eight characters
             for each. Light pen input is possible.

NAME: Texas Sports Data

ADDRESS: Mike Yandell
             P. O. Box 40351
             Fort Worth, Texas 76140

PHONE: (817) 478-4055

HARDWARE: Apple TRS-80

SOFTWARE: $1,500

COMMENTS: This program uses 15 numeric entries of up to 15
             characters to process up to six games. Forty different
             formations may be used. Graphs are used to display
             tendencies on the printout. If you don't wish to
             purchase the software, you may use T.S.D. as a
             scouting service with a guaranteed return time.

NAME: Time Analysis

ADDRESS: Grant Patik
             96 S. Wyoming Avenue
             Buffalo, Wyoming 82834

PHONE: (307) 684-2961

HARDWARE: Apple
             Wang

NAME: Troika System

ADDRESS: 8312 Mariner Court
             Gaithersburg, Maryland 20879

PHONE: (301) 253-4537

HARDWARE: Apple II

SOFTWARE: $75

NAME: The 12th Man

ADDRESS: The 12th Man, Inc.
                1010 Deposit Guaranty Plaza
                Jackson, Mississippi 39201

PHONE: (601) 981-39201

HARDWARE: Kaypro-10
                64 K RAM
                10 MB hard disk storage
                Epson RX-80 printer, 80 or 132 column

SOFTWARE: The 12th Man—offensive and defensive scouting.
                Perfect Calc and Microplan—electronic spreadsheets.
                Wordstar and Perfect Writer—word processing. The
                Word Plus—spelling checker. M-Basic—advanced
                programming applications.

SYSTEM
PRICE: $8,000 (includes all hardware and software)

COMMENTS: This unique package is a complete computer system
                for football scouting and athletic administration. Its
                defensive scouting package allows for the analysis of
                fronts, stunts, dogs, backs, blitzes, and coverage.
                Instruction seminar and 24-hour hot line are
                provided. Future enhancements will include a
                strength development program and dietary program.

WHAT'S IN THE FUTURE

The future of computer analysis of football strategy is exciting. The
following excerpts from two national magazines are enough to whet
the appetite of any football coach looking for a new competitive edge.
In the November, 1982, issue of *Popular Computing*, Allan Zullo reports
in his article, "North Dallas Fortran":

As other teams close the computer gap between themselves and the (Dallas) Cowboys, (Tom) Landry and his assistants are constantly exploring creative new applications for the computer.

Assistant coach Bob Ward and computer consultant Gideon Ariel are tinkering with a program called 'formation analysis.' The computer detects weaknesses in the opposing team based on the position of the player, his physical strength, speed, and reaction time—information gleaned entirely from game films. The computer also simulates how and where the opposing players will move on a given play.

The article "Gideon Ariel, The Guru of Computerized Biomechanical Analysis," which appeared in *Scholastic Coach* in January, 1983, quotes:

Gideon Ariel: 'Yes, we are working with Bob Ward, the training coach (Dallas Cowboys). We believe that formation analysis is in the future of every team. You know how big football is. But ask a coach what he's going to do next week and how certain he is that it will work in a certain situation, and he'll only give you a guess.'

THE LITERATURE

The educational progress of those who use computers is determined by the number of new ideas and varying sources to which they have access. At this point you know more about personal computers and their application to offensive football scouting than do most of the football coaches in this country, because you took the time to read this book. We hope it has supplied you with a strong foundation of important knowledge in the use of personal computers for successful football coaching in the seasons ahead. There is a saying in the football coaching profession to the effect that if you are using yesterday's methods in today's game, you may not have a coaching job tomorrow. After reading this book you are ahead of today's methods for tomorrow's game; so with continued learning you should be in the coaching profession as long as you wish.

However, this book is only a starting point. You must keep up with the rapid changes in personal computer applications in athletics. One way to do this is to review the literature. So far only a few relevant articles have appeared in the athletic periodicals listed here. We expect there will be more in the future.

Athletic Journal, Vol. 61, No. 8, April, 1981, pp. 34–35, 68, "Computerized Scouting," Charles Frazier and Alan Hatfield.

Athletic Journal, Vol. 63, No. 10, May, 1983, pp. 8–13, 63, "Computers: What Every Coach Should Know," Charles Frazier and Alan Hatfield.

Athletic Journal, Vol. 64, No. 1, September, 1983, pp. 38–41, "Coach . . . Scout Thyself!," Jim Finstad.

Coach and Athlete, November, 1976, "Computerized Scouting," Ted Kempski, Barry Streeter.

Coaching Clinic, Vol. 16, No. 4, April, 1978, p. 26, "Computer and Its Use in Football," G. C. Kraft and D. Knapman.

Coaching Clinic, Vol. 16, No. 6, June, 1978, pp. 31–32, "Computer Scouting," G. Hampton.

Scholastic Coach, Vol. 53, No. 3, October, 1983, pp. 52–55, "Everything That Coaches Want to Know About Computers," Jim Finstad.

Texas Coach, Vol. 26, No. 6, February, 1983, p. 40, "Computer Scouting," Ken Kirkham.

Texas Coach, Vol. 27, No. 1, September, 1983, p. 25, "Game Time Opponent Analysis via Microcomputer," Don Knezek.

Texas Coach, Vol. 27, No. 2, October, 1983, pp. 18–19, "Scouting and Analysis," Don Knezek.

A classic book, invaluable for its treatment of scouting procedures, especially in the area of collecting data, is *Football Scouting,* Robert C. MacKenzie, Prentice-Hall, Inc., Englewood, Cliffs, N.J., 1955.

Another fine work which includes a brief overview of computerized scouting is *Football Coach's Complete Scouting and Game Plan Guide,* Bobby Rexrode, Parker Publishing Co., Inc., West Nyack, N.Y., 1983.

FINAL COMMENTS

Coaches should seriously consider using a personal computer for the following reasons:

1. Most likely there already are personal computers in your school's mathematics or science departments which would be available to the coaching staff at no cost. If not, almost any athletic department can afford the cost of a computer today; or it would be a good Booster Club project. The financial barriers to owning one's own computer system have fallen.

2. Your school may have faculty members who are trained in the use of the personal computer. Any school that purchases computers for their students has the foresight to train certain faculty members to teach students how to use these machines. Most of these faculty members would be happy to help coaches learn to use the computer and assist them with any problems they may have. You could also check a nearby computer shop for their night classes, or a neighboring junior college's continuing education curriculum for computer courses.

3. More and more commercially prepared athletic computer programs are coming on the market. Coaches can purchase these at a very nominal cost. Purchase of a program is a one-time expense.

4. The capacity of the computer to store, update, analyze, and use information can be of great value to coaches. The computer is a new and better way to get a time-consuming job done more efficiently. Within minutes you can obtain information it takes other coaches hours to compile. Knowing how to use a computer can help coaches better utilize their valuable time and gain a competitive edge.

5. Computers are easy to learn to operate. They are designed to be run by nontechnical people. No previous experience or knowledge of computers is necessary. However, some instruction and training are necessary, and any apprehensions about using a computer will vanish very quickly with a little practice and experience.

6. We used Apple Computer's Quick File //e program to generate the scouting groups (Printout 3-1), scouting sequence (Printout 3-2), and scouting manual labels (Printout 3-3). Personal Software's VisiCalc program was used to generate the offensive statistics (Printout 10-1 to 10-3). The appendices were typed and continually updated using the Apple Writer II word processing program. Our hardware included an Apple //e personal computer with 64K of RAM, two disk drives, an Apple Monitor II, and an Epson FX-80 printer. Many of the other charts and forms we have presented can also be computerized. We are moving in that direction ourselves, not only in football but also in other areas of athletics.

7. While performing a literature search in the preparation of this manuscript, the authors found over 200 printed citations de-

scribing the use of computers in other areas of athletics. It is obvious to us that the computer is becoming the number one coaching tool of the twentieth century. It is no longer a matter of whether coaches will or will not use a computer. It is now a matter of how, how much, and when.

8. There is a grassroots movement among those interested in the use of the personal computer in athletics known as CCIG (Computer Coaching Interest Group). Anyone interested in becoming a member, receiving a newsletter, attending a clinic, producing athletic software, or purchasing athletic software should contact:

   Dr. Frank M. Downing
   Learning Support Services
   202 West Mitchell Avenue
   State College, PA 16801
   (814) 237-6401

   Dr. Downing is working in the area of computer-enhanced football training, which utilizes the educational as well as the organizational ability of a personal computer through CAI (Computer Assisted Instruction). His CCIG organization has the potential to serve as a national clearing house for all athletic software. This would be a great help to all coaches interested in computerized systems.

9. While searching the literature for articles pertaining to computer use in athletics, we utilized the services of ORBIT (Information Retrieval System) through our own computer.

   This was done on our Apple //e by using a Hayes Micromodem //e and Smartcom I communications software. This created a complete plug-in telecomputing system to receive information from ORBIT.

   By subscribing to ORBIT (Information Retrieval System) a coach can access a data base of citations and abstracts called SPORT, which covers the literature of training, sports medicine, international sports history, and other sports topics. For further information contact:

   ORBIT Information Retrieval System
   SDC Search Service
   2500 Colorado Avenue
   Santa Monica, CA 90406
   (800) 352-6689 in California
   (800) 421-7229 in other states and Canada

10. The majority of football scouting programs available require the coach to enter his data from the keyboard. In the future more suppliers will begin to utilize other input devices with their programs. Mouse, voice recognition, light pen, touch screen, and touch tablet entry are all feasible.

11. Coaches will begin to use the personal computer to draw their opponents' formations, plays, and defensive alignments. As the graphics capabilities of personal computers improve, drawing devices become easier to use, and printers produce hard copies with better resolution, the monitor's screen and the printer's graphics will become as much a part of the coach's life as the chalk board.

APPENDIX A

OTHER ATHLETIC USES OF THE PERSONAL COMPUTER

By now most coaches are familiar with the advantages of a computerized football scouting system. Football coaches have discovered that information that would otherwise take hours to compile manually may be obtained within minutes with a computer. The computer is a powerful machine that will calculate, compile, analyze, summarize, store and retrieve information instantly and accurately. It will also display and print reports.

Although one of the most effective uses of the computer is offensive football scouting, there are many other areas in which the computer can be effectively utilized in athletics.

Following is a brief description of some of the other ways personal computers are being used in athletics today.

SPORTS STATISTICS

In today's competition, you need every minute to think about your coaching program. Statistics are absolutely necessary but keeping them in useful order can be a real chore. The computer can solve this time-consuming, tedious task.

Sports statistics programs will help you improve your team's performance. You will be able to pinpoint which players are being most productive. The statistics may be viewed either on the video screen or on a printed report. Typical programs store and compute all the vital statistics and percentages for every player by game and by season to date. You can analyze a team and individual players by a single game or a whole season. By typing your statistical data into the computer, hundreds of bits of team and individual information are at your fingertips. Software is now available for baseball, basketball, football, soccer, swimming, volleyball, track & field, and most other sports. Many commercial sports statistic programs are on the market today.

ATHLETIC ADMINISTRATION

A well-known athletic director recently said, "If I can't do it on the computer, I don't do it."

This pretty well sums up the value of the computer in athletic administration.

The computer has become indispensable in business. Almost every business office in the nation has utilized computer technology to do a more efficient and effective job. The computer will also soon become indispensable in the athletic administration office. It is the best tool available to the athletic director for upgrading his office and the efficiency of his entire athletic program.

Although the computer is new in athletic administration, athletic directors have developed many applications that have helped them to do their jobs better. Listed are some of these applications:

Eligibility lists	Contracts
Insurance records	Bus schedules
Rosters	Personnel
Awards	Maintenance records
Injury reports	Utility consumption
Game reports	Student aid records
Mailing lists	Recruiting records
Check writing	Work orders
Workers lists	Accounting records
Budgets	Sports information
Inventory control	Athletic services
Grade checks	Public relations
Assignment of volunteers	Scheduling contests
Electronic communications	Contest statistics
League standings	Attendance records
Locker assignments	Assigning officials
Facilities management	

PHYSICAL CONDITIONING

These programs provide the coach with computerized fitness analysis for optimal conditioning during off-season or in-season. Data for each player is evaluated for body composition, flexibility, power, strength and C-R endurance. All data are compared to optimal values and individual recommendations. This allows a coach or trainer to prescribe scientifically designed workouts that are tailored to an individual's strengths and playing requirements. It calculates and prints daily workout routines, produces a statistical analysis, and summarizes and stores individual athletic data.

The computer does all of the statistical work and compiles it in a logical, easy-to-read, informative printout. The report is a definite motivational device for the athlete. He will be constantly aware of where his strength level lies in respect to his team, class, or position. Additionally, the reports give the coach an idea of the continual effectiveness of his program. He has a much more accurate reflection of the individual athlete's and team's strength levels.

COMPUTERIZED EXERCISE EQUIPMENT FOR CONDITIONING AND REHABILITATION

The union of computerization and exercise equipment is the trend of the future. The application of many unique features of computers to the long-established fields of resistive exercise training, rehabilitation, and physical fitness can only benefit such programs.

The underlying principle behind these innovations is that of a computer-controlled feedback which is able to maintain any desired pattern of force and motion throughout the range of each exercise. This patterned progression of resistance results in the optimum training effect.

The advantage of this capability is that the user can select the overall pattern of exercise while the machine assumes responsibility for choosing the precise force level, speed of movement, and temporal sequence to achieve that pattern.

The computer-controlled resistive exercise system represents a new era in physical fitness, physical therapy and athletic training. For the first time, the coach has a training device which can extend his own ability to design a program and allow constant evaluation for enhanced progress.

The Omni-Tron System 1, from Hydra-Fitness Industries, Inc., Belton, Texas, is an important new advancement in the technology of computer-aided conditioning and rehabilitation. The Omni-Tron provides instantaneous, highly accurate measurements of strength, power and endurance, and has the capacity to store this information for comparison to later data in order to efficiently chart the athlete's progress in conditioning and rehabilitation. All measurements are collected by the microprocessor, and fed to the computer, which evaluates and stores them for future use, such as comparisons during stages of a conditioning or rehabilitation program.

BIOMECHANICAL ANALYSIS

Biomechanics is the application of principles from mechanics, engineering, physiology, and anatomy to the study of the human body in motion. It also includes detailed analysis of performance and efforts to improve performance by scientifically improving techniques or equipment. It is designed to provide solutions for the problems of athletic performance. This new technological information can be used to optimize the function of the body in each athletic event. Biomechanical analysis is a sophisticated tool for the coach to use to upgrade technique in sports.

Previously, biomechanical analysis software was only available for larger, expensive computers. Today, software systems have been designed that will run on microcomputers and be able to do what the multimillion-dollar computers did in the past. It is predicted that every athletic program is going to have this kind of system in the foreseeable future.

PLAYER EVALUATION

Before a coach can evaluate a player he must first analyze his or her sport in order to determine what skills or characteristics make for a successful team member. The coach must then rank each of these factors in relative importance and then rate each player on each of the factors. When he puts this information into a computer it does the rest. It weighs each player's strengths and weaknesses, and it prints out, in any given order, a list of the players with scores in each category and a total score. The coach can compare the score of each team member. This gives the coach a rational and demonstrable basis for his action when rating or selecting team members. It is an objective approach to rating players and it encourages athletes to work on their specific problems.

SIMULATION OF GAME SITUATIONS

Computer programs can also be devised to simulate game situations in order to make sure that the athletes understand various offenses and defenses.

A football coach can simulate offensive plays and defensive alignments against various sets and personnel.

With this type of program a coach could put into the computer
each offensive play he wants to run against his opponent. He could
then feed the computer the defense the opposition is most likely to run
in each situation. By punching the right key the coach is able to watch
the play develop on the monitor. After all of his plays have been
assessed against the various defensive fronts, play selection and personnel would be made for the next game.

Coaches and athletic directors will find that the more they use the
computer, the more uses they can find for the computer. The possibilities are almost limitless.

If you are like most coaches you probably do not know where to
find software for athletic uses or even what software is available. Appendix B, an athletic software directory, provides this information.

APPENDIX B

ATHLETIC SOFTWARE DIRECTORY

Company Listing and Program Description

There are many areas in which the computer can be effectively utilized in athletics—all the way from athletic administration to wrestling. A commercial line of software is available for these uses.

The Athletic Software Directory lists 51 software publishing companies that are now offering software programs designed specifically for athletic uses. These programs are easy to use. They are usually menu-driven which means instructions are shown on the screen telling you what to do next.

The directory lists the publisher's address and phone number. Hardware requirements and prices are listed for comparison purposes. A description of each program, based on the promotional material available, is given to allow fast, thorough comparison of programs.

To the best of our knowledge the Athletic Software Directory is the most current and largest compilation of athletic software available to coaches today. It is a comprehensive information source to aid the coach in locating the latest athletic software. It allows fast, thorough comparison of programs and prices.

This directory does not include football scouting software. A directory of football scouting software is included in Chapter 11. It does, however, include software for football statistics and other areas related to football.

The Athletic Software Directory is compiled from advertisements and brochures of athletic software and is published as an information source for coaches who use microcomputers. It is a compilation of numerous application software programs prepared by both professional and amateur programmers. These programs are offered by the vendors listed. All inquiries and correspondence concerning the programs should be directed to the vendor at the address shown in the directory.

The authors have not examined, evaluated or tested the programs offered by other persons, firms, or companies. The authors make no warranties or recommendations, expressed or implied, with respect to these programs, including, but not limited to: availability, accuracy, reliability, capacity of software, performance, hardware requirements, or whether such programs are merchantable and fit for the purpose for which they were intended.

In no event shall the authors be liable for any economic loss or indirect, special or consequential damages by or in connection with the purchase, lease, license, use or operation by any person or entity of any software listed herein. Further, the authors are not responsible for errors occurring in the directory listings and assume no liability for use of information contained in these pages.

The authors suggest that coaches interested in software programs listed contact the company for additional information about current prices, hardware requirements or other information needed.

ATHLETIC SOFTWARE DIRECTORY— PROGRAM DESCRIPTION

1. Academy Hill Press
   RD #2
   Box 357
   Red Hook, NY 12571
   (914) 758-0402

Basketball

Hoops Basketball Statistics

Whether you are a college coach, a senior or junior high school coach, a CYO or city league coach, or even a coach in the Wednesday night men's league—if you have access to an IBM-PC this program can make keeping basketball statistics fun. The program provides you with just about every useful statistic you can think of. You'll get: team statistics of the latest game; cumulative team statistics; personal game statistics; personal cumulative statistics; and game and cumulative personal rankings in each statistic. Further, the Hoops program gives you complete flexibility in deciding which statistic you want to print.

In addition to all the statistical categories you would expect, such as points per game, field goal and foul shooting averages, rebounds, steals, blocked shots, assists, turnovers, and the like, Hoops provides other types of statistics which will be described.

The Hoops printout is generated after you enter the statistics for the latest game. The printout is divided into three sections: team statistics, personal statistics, and personal rankings under each statistic. These three sections are further broken down as follows:

Team Statistics: The team statistics section contains team statistics for the latest game and team cumulative statistics as of the latest game.

Personal Statistics: The personal statistics section contains four types of statistics for the latest game; actual statistics for the latest game; projected statistics for the latest game; cumulative statistics; and Minute-Stats. The actual statistics and cumulative statistics are self-explanatory. However, the projected statistics and the minute-stats require a bit of an explanation.

Projected Statistics: Based on the number of minutes a person plays in the game, the Hoops program projects what that person's statistics would have been if he or she had played the whole game at the same statistical pace he or she attained for the actual minutes played. Projections are calculated for each statistic.

Minute-Stats: The minutes-played statistics are perhaps the most valuable statistics that can be gathered by the coach. They are cumulative statistics, and are computed solely on the number of minutes played as such. They give a "true performance" rating for each of your players over a period of time.

Personal Rankings: The personal rankings section ranks all your players under each statistic. This section lists rankings in the following order: First, the latest game rankings are printed—actual, then projected rankings. Next, the cumulative rankings are printed—totals first, then averages. Finally, minute-stats rankings are listed.

Hoops also provides a "regression rating" which is generated for each individual and totaled for the team. The regression rating is simply a rating of how well the team or individual has done statistically. To get an individual regression rating, the Hoops program gives the player one point for each of the following: each point scored, each rebound, each blocked shot, each assist, and each steal. The Hoops program takes away one point for each turnover. The team regression rating is a total of the individual regression ratings.

To use HOOPS, you must have an IBM personal computer (PC, portable, or XT) with at least 64K of storage. You must also have a monitor, an IBM dot matrix (or compatible) printer, and at least one 320K diskette drive or two 160K diskette drives. In addition you must have some version of DOS and either BASIC or BASICA.

2. American Sports Data
   31 Rockledge Road
   Hartsdale, NY 10530

Track

Quality Mileage Program

Provides a scientific basis for improved running performance. A unique system that tells you what your mileage is really worth. It provides you with a sophisticated method of monitoring your total running effort. By indexing your performance according to pace, running time, and individual ability, the computer converts your mileage into a "quality quotient." The quality mileage program is the product of extensive mathematical and physiological research. By giving you a more refined measure of training intensity, it facilitates precision peaking and tapering. By taking the guesswork out of recovery time, it helps you avoid overtraining and injuries.

Radio Shack TRS-80 MOD III
Diskette $29.95

3. AMTI Biomechanics
   141 California St.
   Newton, MA 02158

Conditioning

Protrain Computerized Exercise Record And Prescription System

Allows a coach or trainer to prescribe scientifically designed workouts that are tailored to an individual's strength and playing requirements. Using the athlete's functional strength data, the Protrain System calculates and prints daily workout routines, produces a statistical analysis and summarizes and stores individual athletic data.

System includes Protrain Software, North Star Horizon microcomputer, display terminal, printer, and floating point board.

4. Anjon Nutritional Analysis System
   P. O. Box 4278
   South Bend, IN 46634
   (219) 233-6695

Conditioning

Anjon Sports Conditioning

It is the first system that integrates all aspects of conditioning:

1. Personnel Management
2. Nutrition
3. Bicycle Ergometry
4. Weight Training
5. Fitness Testing

Personnel Management: Personnel management organizes all the components from nutrition to fitness testing in one file. This eliminates the time spent interpreting charts and record sheets. The information from each component of the Anjon System can be sorted to highlight data for the individual or team, which is beneficial for the success of any conditioning program.

Nutrition: All aspects of sports conditioning are important. To neglect any area or to emphasize only one will typically produce performance levels that are rarely the maximum. Nutrition is one component most programs are unsure about how to control. Anjon can take the uncertainty away for you. They can help you incorporate the nutrition component into your existing program to produce better overall results. The software program produces an easy-to-understand report that actually teaches your athletes how to eat right. It will pinpoint problem areas, as well as encourage the players to continue the good habits they already have.

Bicycle Ergometry: The bicycle ergometry program is used to evaluate an athlete's aerobic capacity. Once this has been determined, you can prescribe exercise intensities that represent a percentage of the player's maximum oxygen uptake. Duration of exercise can be continuous or interval in nature. The exercise prescription can be set up for individual players or the entire team.

Body Composition: Currently, the methods for calculating the percentage of fat and body density range from elaborate techniques, which include hydrostatic weighing, to equations that are reasonable for the coach to administer. With the Anjon System, you can select an equation for a specific population, take the correct measurements and estimate the player's body composition.

Weight Training: The Anjon System can help you develop various cycles for the individual or team. An added feature is the ability to predict Maximum Voluntary Contraction (MCV) from exercise at submaximal loads.

Fitness Testing: There are numerous physical tests for strength, power, endurance, etc. . . The Anjon System has been designed so that the results of these tests can be added to the player's personal file. This gives you the advantages of monitoring the player's progress, determining if the conditioning program is meeting your objectives, and detecting the strong and weak points of the conditioning program.

Anjon Sports Conditioning System, including Rainbow 100+ Computer System, $8,465.00 to $9,365.00. This includes on-site installation and training and 1-year warranty (Hardware & Software). Anjon Sports Conditioning System only, including on-site installation and training and 1-year warranty, $2,450.00.

5. Athletic Computer Programs
   P. O. Box 9146
   College Station, TX 77840
   (409) 696-2921

Administration

Budget

Will prepare your budget for administration, training and up to 20 different sports. The areas for Administration are: Capital, Admin-

istration Supplies, Travel and Other. The areas for Training are Capital, Training Supplies, Travel and Other. The areas for each Sport are Capital, Clothing and Supplies, Team Travel, Coaches' Travel, Officiating, Awards, and Other. There are provisions for 10 Capital Items, 30 Supplies Items, 5 Awards Items and 30 Other items. Each item under each of the areas is that of the user. The program provides worksheets on which to work up the Budget. Items can be added or deleted at any time. Amounts can be changed at any time and will be reflected in the Totals. The program provides totals for Administration, Training and each of the Sports. It also produces a Grand Total.
Price: $59.95.

Inventory

The Inventory program provides for a computerized Inventory System. There is space for 200 Capital Items (items of a permanent nature which may have a serial number and/or a property number assigned by your school). There is space for 600 Non-capital Items (such as uniforms, balls, training supplies, office supplies, etc.). Items can be added or deleted at any time. 20 different Sports are provided for. Each item is coded by Sport, Administration or Training. Inventory list may be run by Sport or Total. The program produces worksheets for each Sport on which to record the physical counts when taking the inventory.
Price: $59.95.

Roster

The Roster program maintains a Master Roster for all of your participants. 20 different Sports are provided and lists can be run by Sport, Class and a Detailed List of all Information for each Student. The Information Maintained: Name, Date of Birth, Address, Home Phone, Parent's Name, Parent's Business Phone, Date Established in District, Class, and Sports participated in. The program will produce Mailing Labels addressed to either the student or parents by Sport, Class or All. There is an Edit Utility to keep the files up to date at all times.
Price: $59.95.
Price for all three: $139.95.

Baseball

Baseball Statistics

Baseball Statistics provides a system for keeping 26 Offensive/Defensive Statistics and 13 Pitching Statistics for 30 players and 10 pitchers for 40 games. The 26 Offensive/Defensive Statistics are: Games Played, at Bat, Hits, Doubles, Triples, Home Runs, Batting Average, Slugging Average, Plate Appearances, On-Base-Fielder's Choice, On-Base-Error, Base on Balls, Hit by Pitcher, On-Base Average, Struckout, Sacrifices, R.B.I., Runs, Stolen Bases Attempted, Stolen Bases, Stolen Base Percentage, Put-outs, Assists, Errors, Passed Balls, and Fielding Average.

The 13 Pitching Statistics are: Pitching Appearance, Won, Lost, Save, Innings Pitched, Runs, Earned Runs, E.R.A., Hits, Base on Balls, Strikeouts, Wild Pitches, and Hit Batters.

Both Team and Individual Statistics are calculated for both Game and Season.
Price $59.95

There is a College version requiring two disks that has a capacity for 40 Players, 20 Pitchers and 80 games.
Price $69.95.

Basketball

Basketball Statistics

Basketball Statistics provides a system to keep 26 Individual Statistics for 20 players for 40 games. The 26 Individual Statistics kept are: Games Played, Field Goals Attempted, Field Goals Made, Free Throws Attempted, Free Throws Made, Assists, Offensive Rebounds, Defensive Rebounds, Steals, Shots Blocked, Personal Fouls, Technical Fouls, Traveling, Double Dribble, 3-Second Violation, 5-Second Violation, Line Violation, Lane Violation, Over and Back, Throw Away, Pass Not Handled, Lost Control, Had Stolen, Tied Up, and Charge.

Calculated Statistics are Field Goal Percentage, Free Throw Percentage, and Averages for Scoring, Assists, Offensive Rebounds, Defensive Rebounds, Steals, Blocks, Personal Fouls, Technical Fouls, and Turnovers.

A worksheet is provided for keeping the statistics during the game and for entering them into the program. Both Team and Individual Statistics are calculated for both game and season.
Price: $59.95.

Football

Football Statistics

The Football Statistics program keeps both Team and Individual Statistics for 16 games. Team Statistics are kept for both you and your opponents. The Individual Statistics are kept for your team only with a capacity of 50 players.

Both Team and Individual Statistics are calculated for both Game and Season. Worksheets are provided to keep the statistics during the game. Team statistical categories are: Game Summary, Scoring, Rushing, Passing, First Downs, Turnovers, Field Goals, Extra Points, Kickoffs, Punts, and Penalties. Individual statistical categories are: Rushing, Passing, Receiving, Scoring, Returns, and Defense.
Price: $69.95 (Two-Disk Program).

Football Play Analysis

Football Play Analysis analyzes your Rushing and Passing Plays. There is room for 80 Rushing and 80 Passing Plays. All plays are in your terminology.

Rushing Plays are ranked by: Calls, Completions, Net Yards, Interceptions, Sacks, Completion Average, Yards per Completion, Interceptions and Sacks per Call. All analysis is done for both individual games and season.
Price: $59.95.

Off-Season Training

Off-season Football

Off-season football is designed to keep a record of your players' off-season progress, analyze their test scores and calculate goals and a workout schedule for 200 players. The system provides for 10 Power/Weightlifting tests and 5 Speed/Skills tests. The number and name of tests you use is your choice. The system operates on a four-week cycle with 12 test periods (12 months). Your players are weighed and tested for each test at the beginning of the test period. A Workout Schedule is provided for each player, calculated on Sets, Repetitions, and Percentages of Test Weights that you provide. An analysis is made based on your standards for each test for each player.
Price: $69.95 (Two Disk Program).

Track and Field

Track and Field Statistics

Keeps your schedule and all statistics (including best performance) for each participant and each event.

All programs are available for the Radio Shack TRS-80 Models III and 4 Computers. Most are available for the Apple II+ and //e. Radio

Shack programs require an 80-column or larger Parallel Printer. Apple programs require an 80-column or larger Parallel Printer, Parallel Card, 80-column card, and a minimum of 64K memory. Both systems require two disk drives for Football Statistics, Off-Season Football and the College version of Baseball Statistics.

6. Big G Software
   Rt 2 Box 111
   Alleyton, TX 78935
   (409) 732-3904

Baseball Statistics

Computerized Baseball Statistics

Similar to Basketball Statistics (below), keeps 30 statistical items consisting of the usual items plus on-base avg., fielding avg, and contact avg.

Basketball Statistics

Computerized Basketball Statistics

Keeps individual and team stats for the entire year for all teams; current game, season to date, and conference to date including:

FG Attempts	Defensive Rebounds
FT Attempts	Charges Taken
Total Points	FG Percentages
Offensive Rebounds	FT Percentages
Turnovers	Steals
FG Made	Total Rebounds
FT Made	Blocked Shots
Assists	

Requires: Radio Shack TRS80 MOD III or 4, Apple II+ or //e Computer
   48K RAM—1 disk drive—132 Column Printer
   Works with all Epson and most Radio Shack printers
   $39.95 plus $2.00 shipping

7. Body Enterprises, Inc.
   P. O. Box 80577
   Lincoln, NE 68501
   (402) 466-8877

Conditioning

Athletic Index Software Package

The athletic index software package enables you to score a battery of field tests similar to the scoring of the decathlon. Each test you select is given a total of 1,000 points that can be scored. The program then gives a composite score of all the tests. An overall athletic index helps you determine who your best athletes are, and a weight index helps you to determine athletic ability by handicapping body weight.

Besides scoring your athletes, you can also use the athletic index to do the following:

1. To make comparisons with other athletes according to age, sex, size, and position.
2. To aid in the construction of training programs.
3. To file, sort, merge, and do statistical analysis of testing data.
4. To evaluate the effectiveness of your training program.
5. To motivate your athletes.

This package, written for Apple or Apple compatible computers, includes:

1. Program disks.
2. User guide.
3. Testing guide.

Strength Disk

This software package is designed for an entire athletic program. Every coach in your school can become an instant strength coach. The program is sophisticated, yet very simple to use. By following a documentation brochure, each coach enters in the program that is best for his or her particular sport. Then the coach enters the appropriate data, and prints out a lifting cycle for each athlete's individual program. Adjustments can be made until the program is specifically what each coach wants.

The Strength Disk allows you to design individualized programs for large groups, where it wasn't practical in the past. Each athlete can be monitored, and have his workouts adjusted so that he is in peak condition when the competitive season starts, and can maintain his strength as the season progresses. Your athletes no longer have to guess what poundages to use, instead they will be motivated to keep up with the pace of the workouts you have prescribed for them.

The Strength Disk is designed for the Apple line of computers. It is necessary to have 64K of memory for the program to run. In addition, an 80-column printer is required for printing out the individual programs. A version for IBM will be available. Price $495.00.

8. Brock Computer Services
   1226 Booth Street
   Howell, MI 48843
   (517) 546-1075

Bowling

Bowling Secretary

Compiles, update, edits, and prints weekly sheets for bowling leagues. Bantam, Junior, Senior, and Regular leagues. Checks for and prints over average awards. Up to 22 teams and up to 7 members per team. Substitutes recorded and printed (on request). Automatic lane scheduling. Automatic handicap calculation. Prints league name, establishment name, president, and secretary information. Three different print formats for teams and members. Multiple or single copies. Mixed league capability. Team, Individual, Men's, Women's high series and games. (3 levels) with or without handicaps. Weekly message capability. Stores total games, total pins, average, high series, and high game for each team and member. Computes and prints team standings. Total pins are considered.

System requirements: Disk BASIC, 32K RAM, disk drive, and a line printer.
Price: $48.50.

9. C Q Data Systems, Inc.
   P. O. Box 20329
   Raleigh, NC 27619
   (919) 848-3554

Basketball

B-Bas Basketball Analysis System

B-Bas can be operated by one person working from code sheets, game film, or even live action. In less than an hour, your current statistician can learn to operate the system. Computer will calculate all the following reports on both you and your opponent:

Official Game Scoresheet: Individual and team totals, team shotting percentages by period, team rebounding stats, individual minutes played, score by periods, assists and much more.

Comparison of Team Performance: Each team is compared by numerous statistics, including field goal percentages, free throw percentages, offensive and defensive rebounding percentages, the number of offensive and defensive fouls committed, the number of times a team scores following a turnover by its opponent, a grading system for the team and more.

Analysis of Player Performance: Every statistic contained in the team performance report is provided on an individual player basis. A player grading system and stats describing overall team performance while a particular player is in the game are also included.

Defensive Effectiveness Report: A comparison of each defense played by both teams during the game is provided. It includes the points per possession, shooting percentages, rebounding percentages, turnover rates and much more against each defense faced. All of these reports can be completed on a single game basis or on any combination of games. For instance, you may want your year-to-date totals, your conference game totals, your home and away totals or any other combination.

B-Bas Plus Basketball Analysis System

B-Bas Plus has all the reports listed above for the B-Bas System, plus two additional reports:

Lineup Combination Analysis: This report provides information to the coach on every lineup combination used in a game or over the course of the season. How well each lineup is performing as a unit is displayed in terms of its shooting percentage, rebounding percentage, turnover rate, assist rate and more.

Lineup By Defense Analysis: This report builds upon the previous one by taking the lineups and displaying them against each defense they faced. At this point a coach can see how well each of his lineups has played against a man-to-man, a 2-3 zone, pressure defense or whatever they have faced. As a scouting tool, the report provides the same information on your opponent. You will be able to tell which of your defenses worked particularly well against which of your opponent's lineups. B-Bas and B-Bas Plus have both single and multiple game capabilities.

B-B Stats Basketball Statistical System

A low-cost statistical program that enables the user to enter end-of-game stats and produces two reports for individual games: The Official Scoresheet and a Summary of Individual and Team Averages/Percentages. Stats may be combined for any games selected such as season, home games or conference games. In addition, B-B Stats stores information on the team's schedule and record. It was designed to aid statisticians and sports information directors develop and maintain accurate and timely reports for the game of basketball. B-B Stats also calculates averages and percentages for individual players and for the team.

Football

F-B Stats Football Statistical System

F-B Stats is a low-cost statistical system designed to summarize the game of football.The system provides the user with a comprehensive set of statistics for individual games and for multiple games. It provides comprehensive team and individual stats, ranks players in order within each statistical category, calculates multiple game averages, and maintains information on the team schedule and record.

Off-Season Training

Strength Manager

Designed to enable coaches to store a large amount of information on each athlete involved in a strength program, measure his/her progress, and produce daily/weekly/monthly workout schedules. Program instructs coach on how to devise schedules for repetitions and weights. Athletes can then be assigned to various weight stations and given schedules which will best accomplish their specific goals. The task of designing and assigning training schedules becomes a fast and simple operation. The coach and the athlete are provided with printed reports of the workout schedule designed specifically for the athlete.

Recruiting

Recruit Manager

This program was designed to aid coaches in handling the large amount of information they keep on potential recruits. Recruit manager will store the information you want maintained on a recruit and allow you quick and easy access to it.

Apple II+ & Apple //e
80-Column Card—All input routines in 40 columns—output in 80 columns.

Can also be adapted for use on several other computer systems—contact company.

10. Champs, Inc.
P. O. Box 24054
Apple Valley, MN 55124
(612) 432-4072 or (612) 884-8999

Administration

CHAMPS/A—Schedules/Calendars/Contracts

Champs systems standardize data collection, handle information accurately and eliminate time-consuming report typing. Regardless of the size of your school, Champs will let you gather data more effectively, process it quickly and get timely, accurate reports. You only handle data once.

Suppose your job requires scheduling 800-1,000 athletic/activity events per year.

1. Using preprinted coding forms, CHAMPS/A shows you how to gather scheduling data that's immediately ready for computer input.

2. With the Master Schedule Summary Sheet, you can quickly identify potential open dates and conflicts in your schedule.

3. CHAMPS/A is a complete system that lets you record, file, store, review, change, retrieve and report virtually every detail pertaining to events at your school.

4. The computer automatically prints out up-to-date and accurate reports whenever you need them. Reports include:

1. Program Schedules*
2. Calendars of Events*
3. Requests for Home Event Workers.
4. Requests for Home Event Officials.
5. Contracts for Scheduled Events.
6. Contracts for Scheduled Officals.

*Program and calendar report options include: Home and/or Away Events; Events at Specified Playing Sites; Events by Specified Opponent; Athletic and/or Non-Athletic Events.

CHAMPS/E—Eligibility/Rosters/Directory

1. CHAMPS/E provides the complete system for maintaining up to 25 items of information on every student in your program.

2. Information pertaining to eligibility, rosters, directories, awards, fees, equipment and more is entered on pre-printed coding forms.

3. Student eligibility information only needs to be entered on the computer once, no matter how many sports or activities a student participates in.

4. CHAMPS/E contains all the programming necessary to quickly create virtually any type of updated report that you want. Here are some examples:

1. Master Eligibility Lists
2. Team Rosters
3. Directory Information
4. Letters and Awards Reports
5. Fee Reports
6. Equipment Reports

You can create reports using as few or as many items as you need.

In seconds, CHAMPS/A and CHAMPS/E automatically print the kind of reports you expect from the neatest, most efficient secretary. Important, accurate, and updated information can be communicated to coaches, staff, parents, and officals.

Recruiting

CHAMPS/R—Recruiting Management System

1. Supports the *Data Gathering Process* through the use of a pre-designed Coding Form, allowing you to gather a complete data profile on each recruit.

2. Helps you *organize the people* in your recruiting management system.

3. Supplies you with a *Menu of Composite Reports* on Recruits that are printed automatically, according to your specifications:

Overall Composites
Composites By Positions
Composites By Recruiter
Composites By Recruiter And Position

4. These reports will *assist you in Managing and evaluating* a large quantity of personnel data.

5. Allows you to *create "Custom" Reports* that cross-match specific data on recruits, identify recruits that satisfy minimum/maximum criteria that you establish, and sort specific data.

CHAMPS operates on these computers:

Apple II microcomputer (64K) and monitor with two disk drives and any printer capable of 132 characters per line.

TRS-80 Model III 48K microcomputer two-disk system with any Radio Shack 132-column line printer.

11. Cherrygarth Farms Software, Inc.
101 South Dewey St.
Auburn, IN 46706
(219) 925-1093

Baseball

Baseball Records

The program has two parts for data entry. These contain the offensive, defensive, and pitching information. The appropriate calculations are made when and where they are needed. Calculations are made on an individual game basis and can be seen at this time. Accumulated totals and averages are calculated and shown when the reports are written.

The reports generated by the program are such that the record of any player or players, game or games can be produced at any time with the correct, up-to-date accumulated totals and averages.

Basketball

Basketball Records

This program can be used for keeping statistics for every player for every game. It can be used for any number of different teams within a school. It can be used for scouting an opponent.

A school needs to have available to the press and for their own needs the game statistics, up-dated player and team averages and totals as soon as possible after the game.

This program will do that. It is possible to generate reports on any player or players, game or games at any time. All accumulated totals and averages will be correct for the player or players, game or games for the season to date.

Data entry for each player for each game is a maximum of 23 entries. These are divided into 13 offensive and defensive entries and 10 opponent offensive entries.

Comparisons are made between the player and his opponent. If this much detail is not needed, the coach simply leaves out those parts that are not needed in that situation.

Football

Football Records

Probably no coach keeps more information on more athletes than the football coach. The time spent in this aspect of the game by either the coaching staff, student assistants, or adult helpers shows the importance placed on this information.

This program is meant to simplify or streamline that time factor and yet have all the necessary information readily available for those who need it. Because of the large volume of information collected, data entry into the program is broken down into two sections. Offensive data has 16 entries. The defensive/kicking data also has 16 entries. Numerous calculations are made in each section.

The reports are such that records for any player or players, game or games, can be produced at any time. The accumulated totals and averages for both the individual and team will be up-to-date regardless of what game or player was selected.

Track and Field

Track and Field

Keeping accurate data on individuals who participate in track and field helps a great deal in evaluating their performance over the course of a season. This program will help the coach keep up-to-date records and placings on both the individual and relay efforts.

Data entry allows for meet points, times, distances, and placings of each individual for each meet. Total points are calculated for the individual meets and are accumulated for the season. No comparison is made concerning times and distances from one meet to another. All individual and relay events are metric. The individual can have data entry in any event in any meet.

The reports produced by the program allow for the records of any player or players, meet or meets, to be generated at any time.

These programs include a manual, a program disk and a data disk. It can be used on either a single or dual disk drive. The data disk

can be copied easily so that a different data disk can be used for every team and back-up copies can be made.
Price: $49.95 each.

System requirements: Apple II Plus, Apple //e, 48K: DOS 3.3, Single or Dual Disk Drive.

12. Comp-U-Sports, Inc.
     P. O. Box 1340
     Frederick, MD 21701
     (301) 663-3257

Baseball

Baseball Statistics

Baseball Statistics helps a coach keep track of individual and team statistics including hitting, pitching and fielding. Statistical reports can be generated for individual games as well as for the season.

Basketball

Basketball Stats

Basketball Stats allows a coach or statistician to maintain records for up to 18 players for up to 30 games per season. Individual game and season totals are provided in eleven statistical areas, including both offensive and defensive statistics. For added flexibility, four additional statistics can be defined by the user.

Football

Computer Enhanced Football Training—CEFT

CEFT enables a coach to teach football via the computer, thus maximizing player learning and performance. CEFT is a family of products dealing with the mental side of football. Now you can choose between two products—50 Defense vs. The Pass and 50 Defense vs. The Run. Both contain six lessons with animated and static graphics including: Defensive Goals, Principles, End Play, Perimeter Play, Linebacker Play and Down Lineman Play.

Track and Field

Track and Field Statistics

Track and Field Statistics enables track and field coaches to have vital team and individual participant and single meet and cumulative statistics quickly and easily. It gives you meet data, team and individual scoring, five places for all high school, college and indoor events, split times, records broken and participant ranking. It charts individuals progress for up to 60 participants and 20 meets.

Additional software from Comp-U-Sports includes:

Bowling League Secretary
Football Statistics
Golf Handicapping
Ice Hockey Stats
Player Evaluation
Runner's Log
Soccer Statistics
Volleyball Stats

Compu-U-Sports also offers their SPORTS-PAK. It includes the following software packages:

Easy-Scout (Computerized Football Scouting System)
CEFT (Computer Enhanced Football Training)
Baseball Statistics
Basketball Stats
Track and Field Statistics

SPORTS-PAK includes all 5 of the above programs plus your choice of any two from the above additional list. Price for SPORTS-PAK: $299.00.

Compu-U-Sports GRID-PAK includes:

Easy Scout
CEFT
Football Statistics

Price of GRID-PAK: $199.00

System Requirements: Apple //e and Apple //c.

13. Competitive Computing, Inc.

15 Sequoia Drive
Watchung, NJ 70760
(201) 755-4309

Baseball

Diamond IX Baseball Statistics

It is designed specifically to provide a report of the following:
1. Each player's statistics for each game with the team totals at the bottom.
2. Each player's statistics cumulative for all games played with the team totals at the bottom. It provides the following list of statistics:

At bat	Assists	Strikeouts
Doubles	Slugging percentage	Percentage on base
RBI	Runs	Errors
Att. stolen bases	Triples	Hits
Walks	Batting average	Home runs
On base	Sacrifice	Stolen bases
Hit by pitch	Total at bat	Put outs
Fielding average		

Pitching Statistics

A supplement to the Diamond IX Program.

Basketball

Basketball Statistics

The program includes the following:

Field goals made	Assists
Field goals attempted	Minutes played
Percentage of field goals	Cumulative turn overs
Free throws made	Personal fouls
Free throws attempted	Turn overs
Percentage of free throws	Games played
Rebounds	Cumulative points made
	Average points per game

Apple II
32K with printer and disk drive
$39.95 Plus $2.00 Postage/Handling
Pitching Statistics $9.95 with Diamond IX, $15.95 alone Plus $2.00 Postage/Handling.

14. Compu-Stats
    321 Woodland Dr.
    South Lyon, MI 48178

Basketball

Basketball Statistics

The basketball statistics program was designed to make the job of recording statistics easier. It computes all the averages and totals for single games and keeps track of the season's totals for both the individual player and the team. Along with recording the home team stats, it keeps track of the opposing team's statistics, which makes for easy scouting. The basketball stat program makes the job of keeping stats much easier because it does all the organizing for you. It does all the recording, and it does all the printing out of the stats in neat table form. The user does not need to know anything about computers because the program is written in such a way that it is very difficult to make mistakes.

Written by Steve Case
Includes diskette and complete instructions
$35.00

15. Compu Tech
    Patrick I. Coyne
    2412 Wildwood Drive
    Woodward, OK 73801
    (405) 254-2254

Football

Football Offensive Statistical Package

Designed for capturing play-by-play action in a press box environment and provides for rapid access to printed quarterly as well as final games, individual and team statistical reports.

Software is menu driven—written in CBASIC and designed for individual play data entry for both teams and the compilation and printing of cumulative "quickie" stats by quarter and final comprehensive stats for both individual and team categories. The program logic follows NCAA rules and the statistical reports conform to standard NCAA format.

Osborne 1A or Osborne Executive
Will in theory run on any CP/M based computer
$500.00
Includes operator's manual
Also sells Osborne computer and printer

16. Computer Programs Unlimited
    Sports Division
    5614 Innsbruck
    Bellaire, TX 77401
    (713) 665-6007

Baseball

Baseball-Offense/Defense and Pitcher Statistical Programs

Two separate programs on one disk. Offense/Defense computes
and stores all statistics and percentages for every player for the entire
season. Prints out entire season's statistics by player or by team. Percentages for each player are displayed immediately upon entering
data. Disk also includes a pitcher program which will compute and
store all statistics and percentages for each pitcher for the entire season. $195.00 Plus $3.00 Shipping/Handling.

Basketball

Basketball Statistical Program

Stores and computes all statistics and percentages for every player for the entire season. Prints out the entire season by player or by
team. $175.00 Plus $3.00 Shipping/Handling.

Apple II+ or Apple //e
Printer-Epson MX-80 Can be used without a printer.

17. Computer Recovery, Inc.
    Rt. 4 Box 860
    Alvarado, TX 76009
    (817) 783-2208

Baseball

Baseball Analysis

Batting, fielding, and pitching are separated into their own separate areas for individual analysis. Along with up-to-the-minute game

totals come season totals and game averages. Pitcher per-game averages are also given.

Basketball

Basketball Analysis

The basketball analysis allows the up-to-date summary of a player and a team. You can analyze a team and individual players by a single game or a whole season. The basketball program also evaluates each player and a grade is determined on a scale of 100 percent.

Off-Season Training

Off-Season Analysis

Statistics are kept for each player and the total team. After a while you re-analyze your team members and update the computer. The computer will show each individual's progress in eight different areas. A before starting stat and an after statistic is listed. The percentage of improvement, positive or negative, is listed. You also receive the overall percentage of improvement for each player. At the end of your printout will be the team analysis. The team average before and after in each area is listed along with the overall team improvement percentage.

The system comes complete with all documentation.

18. Computerized Football Aids
    P. O. Box 114
    Arlington Heights, IL 60006
    (312) 577-7816

Baseball

Baseball Statistics

A. Records the following: At bats, singles, doubles, triples, home runs, hits, batting average, slugging average, sacrifice hits, walks, putouts, assists, innings pitched, hits given up, strikeouts, runs given up, runs scored, earned run average.

B. Calculates game totals, season total for both the individual and team.

C. Flexible output under the control of the user.
$29.95

Basketball

Basketball Statistics

Similar to baseball stats, except it keeps field goal attempts, field goals, FG percentage, foul tries, fouls made, foul percentage, points, rebounds, personals, technicals, assists.
$29.95

Football

Football Inventory

Keeps track of name, address, phone, locker number, locker combination, and all common personal equipment such as shoulder pads, helmets, etc. Twenty-two entries in all.
$29.95

Quarterback Trainer

Let your quarterback run your plays against defenses you have selected.

You program in the offense:

Offensive Sets
    5 backfield sets
    Right and left formations
    3 quick receivers
    4 quick receivers

Pass Patterns
    3-man patterns
    4-man patterns
    Back releases out of backfield
    Select each receivers route
    You name the pattern

You program in the defense
    Name the defense
    Select the down men
    Shift front right or left
    Select the linebackers
    Shift linebackers right or left
    Six secondary coverages

Realistic
    Computer calls plays and defense
    Defense moves

QB can be sacked
Sound effects
Interceptions
Deflections
Completions
<u>Instructive</u>
Keeps score
Prints out results
Records results for coaches
Indicates which receivers were open

Apple II 48K, 3.3 DOS only—not adaptable to other computers.
$39.95

Stats I Football Statistics

Offense

Total carries	Pass had int (PHI)
Yards gained rush	Yards int returned
Pass attempts	Yards fumbles
Pass completions	Points
Yards gain pass	Xtps
Passes caught	Field Goals
Yards gained rec.	

Defense and Kicking

Tackles	No. of punts
Assists	Total yards punted
Fumbles caused	No. of punt returns
Fumbles recovered	Yards punts returned
Interceptions	No. of kick off returns
Yds run w/int	Kick off return yards

Requires 48K Apple 3.2/3.3 DOS $29.95

Off-season Training

Strength Recorder

A. Projects maximum lifts using a formula developed at the University of Michigan.

B. You can select the lifts you want to record.

C. You can add and edit an existing file.

D. You can sort the data by name or lift.

E. You can update all lifting entries.

$29.95

Apple II and IIe

19. Cramer Educational Services
    Department
    Football Fit-N-Dex
    P. O. Box 1001
    Gardner, KS 66030
    (913) 884-7511

Conditioning

Fit-N-Dex Football Conditioning Software

Fit-N-Dex uses measurements of strength, power, endurance, flexibility and body composition to evaluate fitness of players by age, position and body weight and compares this data to optimum performance characteristics.

You can use the Fit-N-Dex to evaluate a player's fitness profile against the norms of football players of the same age and position. This is an objective aid to player selection, position selection and a personalized training regimen. Most important, the Fit-N-Dex will let you assess each player's actual conditioning levels against his potential to maximize his team contribution.

The Fit-N-Dex will also help you minimize injuries. The computer analysis will help detect weakness among individual players that could lead to less than peak performance or even injury. The computer not only gives you an individual player analysis, it suggests specific exercises to overcome deficiencies.

Another important use of Fit-N-Dex is as a motivational tool. You can instruct the computer to sort team data by individual rankings in strength, flexibility and endurance. For example, the computer could rank all linemen from strongest to weakest in the bench press. These reports can be easily updated as your training progresses.

Fit-N-Dex operates on any Apple II, Apple II+, Apple //e or compatible computer.

Fit-N-Dex software was designed by an exercise physiologist for an NFL team and was adapted for college and high school athletes in a joint venture with Cramer Products. Price: $195.00.

20. Datascore
P. O. Box 995
Sharon, PA 16146

Bowling

Bowlstat 2.5

Bowlstat 2.5 is the latest version of a comprehensive software package which performs most of the statistical record-keeping done by a bowling league secretary. Bowlstat consists of two main programs called Leagstat and Leagrun. Leagstat is used to create a league data file on disk for each bowling league being handled. When Leagstat is run you will be asked to select the league's scoring rules for team and player handicaps, team points, blind scores, etc. and the team and player names and other league information. A complete summary of the league data file can then be printed for reference and error-checking.

The program Leagrun is used to enter scores each week and update the league data file. Entering scores is very simple and error detection built into the program eliminates the need for tedious double checking of keyboard entries.

A third program called Report can be used at any time to print out a listing of all the players in the league, along with their statistics.

TRS-80 Model I, III, IV—$79.95 Model II, 12, 16—$119.95
Requires at least one disk drive, 48K of memory, and a printer.

21. DataStrike
P. O. Box 1148
Franklin Park, IL 60131
(312) 595-6066

Bowling

Bowling Tournament Records

Handles up to 2,000 bowlers. Prior to start of the tournament, enter names of pre-registered bowlers. A number will be assigned at this time to each bowler which will be your access to that bowler. Those bowlers not pre-registered may be entered when entering scores. Enter the event's scores in any order. It calculates all event's scores. Sorts men and women separately if a mixed tournament. Team printouts give team name in expanded print and then lists team players, their scores, handicaps and team series. List of bowlers may be run either alphabetically or numerically. Bowlers listed with handicaps.

   Designed for: IBM
         Apple
         TRS-80
         & Compatibles

22. Educational Activities, Inc.
  P. O.Box 392
  Freeport, NY 11520
  (516) 223-4666

Basketball

Basketball Statistics

  A unique record-keeping program that will allow the coach to follow the statistics on his players and team. Easy to run, the program permits the input of data in approximately 20 categories including:

Field goals attempted	Balls lost
Field goals made	Jump balls gained
Free throws attempted	Jump balls lost
Free throws made	Defensive errors
Offensive rebounds	Charging fouls
Defensive rebounds	Total personal fouls
Steals	Take a charge
Violations	Fast break
Bad passes	Assist
Turnovers	Minutes played

  The program is menu-driven and it is easy to update player and team records or to get current statistics immediately. Player starts may be viewed by season or game. Output is either to a screen for immediate visibility or to a printer for hard copy. Each coach will find that this program greatly speeds his record-keeping, sharpens his knowledge of each player, and helps his decision-making. $59.00

Conditioning

Physical Evaluation Program (P.E.P.)

  The P.E.P. program's four computer programs gives you a structured scientific method of assessing the physical condition of students (and adults too) and enables you to prescribe and monitor progress. A management system saves student records for later comparison and evaluation. The programs are:

Body Composition
Coronary Heart Disease Risk Factors
Life Point Monitoring System

The coach's guide describes the way to administer the program to students and also outlines means of involving parents if desired. It gives explicit directions for taking blood pressure and skinfold or body measurements. It details how to do the step test and how to recognize signs of over-exertion.
$109.00
Apple
Radio Shack TRS-80
Includes back-up diskette

23. Educational Data Systems, Inc.
    P. O. Box 8172
    Mobile, AL 36689
    (205) 344-4781

    Educational Data Systems has the following programs available:

    Athletic Management
    Baseball Statistics
    Basketball Statistics
    Football Statistics
    Scheduling
    Softball Statistics
    Swimming Statistics
    Track Statistics

    Anyone can operate these programs. No computer experience is needed. All data is backed up. Special features may be available on request.

    Radio Shack TRS-80 and Apple $39.95, Minimum 1 disc system.
    IBM PC $59.95

24. Galagar Software
    Box 11A
    Plevna, KS 67568

Basketball

Basketball Statistics

Your team will become more conscious of improving in the areas of shooting percentage, rebounds, steals, assists, and turnovers as they follow the game and accumulated statistics through the season.

Prints and stores statistics in 15 categories for each of the following: 1. Individual, 2. Individual accumulated, 3. Team, 4. Team accumulated, 5. Opponent, 6. Opponent accumulated.

Up to 35 games may be stored on disk. Fifteen minutes from start to finish, it will enter your game's stats, perform more than 200 calculations, print the paper copy (including all game and accumulated statistics) and store the game and accumulated stats on the disk.

> Apple II+ Apple //e
> Radio Shack Model III, IV
> Includes Manual, Stats Sheet, Shot Chart, Notebook
> $50.00 Plus $2.00 for Postage & Handling

25. H & H ADP Security
    P. O. Box 5095
    Falls Church, VA 22044
    (703) 237-7927

Bowling

Bowling League

The bowling program consists of a series of routines designed to accomplish many redundant tasks for the bowling league secretary. It has been configured to enable each individual league to customize the program to its own specific needs. Error routines or verification prompts are used extensively in all areas of the program.

Entering league scores is designed around a two-competing-team configuration. The display employs concise English statements or instructions for entering any data. The amount of league data necessary in league competition has been reduced to team number, member number and three raw scores. Each bowler entered is displayed on the screen under his/her team in a score-sheet format. As each game raw score is entered, it is immediately displayed in the appropriate column in the format. Depending on the type of scoring rule selected, the final computed win/loss points and scores for the two teams are displayed in a score-sheet format.

If history records are to be maintained, the appropriate game data is automatically recorded for each week. In addition, both team and member statistical data such as high game, high series are revised each week.

There are a variety of reports and listings that may be desired during the league's existence. Besides league standings, some of the other types available are; team with membership, or league membership and history records. Usually, a league requires or desires a sort on specific statistics (i.e., High Game Scratch or High Game Handicap) to determine eligibility for league awards. There are 16 sort listings available to the operator on such categories as High-Game Scratch, High-Game-Handicap, High-Average, etc. This program has eliminated much of the sorting time required to list these categories.

The program can accommodate totally separate rules for men and women within a league. This includes not only the scratch, but blinds, absentee and top bowler criteria.

The Bowling program Version 3.0 is available for lease on a Model II TRS-80 Computer for a one time fee of $350.00. The minimum system configuration is 64K with two floppy disk drives or one hard disk and any equivalent Radio Shack printer.

26. Hancock Techtronics Inc.
     101 E. Main Street
     Hancock, MD 21750

Golf

Golf Handicapping System

Hancock Techtronics entered the golf handicapping system in 1977 with the advent of the Radio Shack Model I. In 1981, the system was completely redesigned for the Model II and III with speed and maximum efficiency in operation, storage and sorting of data. The Model II system can store up to 1100 golfers on a one-disk system the Model III 48K can hold up to 300 on one disk and 800 on a two-drive system. The Model II system will operate on Model 12 and 16 and the Model III system will operate on the Model IV system.

The new version of this system allows the flexibility of multiple golf courses with either nine or eighteen holes. The option is also provided to allow the entering of the golfer's scores as they come in from outside courses.

The system files the latest twenty differentials and chooses the appropriate number of the lowest scores to calculate and record the handicap. The course rating for a particular game is also retained to allow future printing of game scores.

Description of Printouts:

1. The records will be printed with name, handicap, number of games this year and all scores on record with asterisks to indicate which scores were used to calculate the handicap.
2. Identical except golfers are printed in golfer number order. A 132-column printer is required.
3. The record will be printed with golfer name, handicap, games on record, and remarks. The printout is done on typewriter size paper.
4. Prints labels with name, handicap, league, date, average differential, number of games played. To be carried by golfer.
5. Prints golfers in order of most improved.
6. Prints golfers in order of lowest handicappers.
7. Prints formatted sheets to post golfers net scores.
8. Enter league name to head printouts.
9. Sorts at convenience of computer operator.

The Model II system is priced at $495.00 and the Model III system is $295.00 plus $3.00 shipping.

27. Hydra-Fitness Industries
    2121 Industrial Blvd.
    P. O. Box 599
    Belton, TX 76513
    1-800-433-3111-U.S.A.
    1-800-792-3031-Texas

Conditioning & Rehabilitation

Omni-Tron System I

Provides you with instantaneous, precise measurements of strength, power, and endurance, and the capacity to store this information for comparison to later data in order to efficiently chart the subject's progress in either conditioning or rehabilitation.

The Omni-Tron System, due to its versatility and durability, works effectively for school/university/professional coaching staffs, therapists, athletic trainers, physiologists, and physicians—anywhere there is a need for testing, evaluation, or research in therapy or conditioning.

Omni-Tron System is comprised of Apple //e computer console, Apple Dot-Matrix printer, digital display monitor and one-disk drive. Each computer is capable of storing records for up to 150 athletes.

28. Instant Software, Inc.
Dept RS-2
Peterborough, NH 03458
(603) 924-7296

Bowling

Bowling League Statistics System

This program keeps a computerized list of league data, team data and data for each bowler. It provides for starting a new league, running a league meet, scoring options, handicapping options, weekly scores, team rank, team scores, individual leaders, league statistics and more.

Radio Shack TRS-80
Model I & III Level II 48K PMC Compatible

29. Korney Board Aids
P. O. Box 264
Roxton, TX 75477
(214) 346-3269

Basketball

B-Ball-Stats

Complete game and season stats printed and ready for your use. With "B-Ball-Stats" you will have a better understanding of your team's strong points as well as its weak areas. Figures game and season averages in minutes instead of hours.

B-Ball-Stats is designed for both the experienced and upcoming dedicated coaches. Typed, organized and ready for you, radio broadcasters, television announcers and college recruiters scouting your players.

B-Ball-Stats includes:

Field Goals Made	Bad Passes
Field Goals Att	Violations
Field Goal %	Fumbles
Free Throws Made	Games Played
Free Throws Att	Recov./Steals
Free Throw %	Assists
Game Points	Quarters
Total Points	Turnovers
Points Avg	All Averages
Off. Rebounds	Def. Rebounds
Rebound Avg	Total Revounds
Total Game Rebounds	Players Game Worth
Playing Time Game	Players Season Worth
Playing Time Season	

Equipment needed: An Apple II, or II+, or //e with 3.3 DOS disk drive or TRS 80 III, or comparable equipment. TRSDOS necessary. Also needed are television monitor and printer adaptable to computer. Delivered Price: $54.95.

Football

Football Stats

Saves time. Gets an edge on your opponent. Gets more information faster for you. Produces complete, neat game reports. With Football Stats you will have a better understanding of your team's strong points as well as its weak areas. Figures game and season averages in minutes instead of hours.

Football Stats is designed for both the experienced and upcoming dedicated coaches. Typed, organized and ready for you, radio broadcasters, television announcers and college recruiters scouting your players.

Football Stats includes:

1. Names and Scoring	(5 Areas)
2. Passing Data	(7 Areas)
3. Rushing Data	(9 Areas)
4. Kicking Data	(9 Areas)
5. Kick Return Data	(8 Areas)
6. Pass Receiving	(4 Areas)
7. Individual Scoring	(7 Areas)
8. Defensive Team	(9 Areas)

9. Offensive Data	(11 Areas)
10. Opponents Team	(37 Areas)

Equipment needed: Apple II, or II+, or //e with 3.3 DOS disk drive. Also needed are television monitor and adaptable printer to computer.
Delivered Price: $59.95.

30. Market Computing
    P. O. Box 6245
    Huntington Beach, CA 92615
    (714) 953-8722

Administration

Athletic Package

This is a 3-disk record-keeping and scheduling package made up of League Standings, League Scheduling, and Reservations. The Reservations program is available in two configurations: Short-Term and Long-Term. Cost for the Athletic Package is $250.00. Any of the above programs may also be purchased separately for $100.00 each.

League Standings: Registers game results and computes standings for one or more leagues. Features:

1. Records win-loss, ties, percentages, games behind, points scored and points given up.
2. Prints mailing labels for all coaches in a given league.
3. Designed for use with league scheduling using common data disk.

Each data disk handles:

1. 400 teams
2. 50 leagues
3. Max. 26 teams if used with League Scheduling

League Scheduling: Creates a round-robin schedule for one or more leagues.
Features:

1. Prepares a game schedule with teams, times and days per week.

2. Allows adjustment for days that the league will not play.
3. Allows adjustment of schedule for times that a particular team cannot play.
4. Allows entry of field assignments for inclusion on the printed schedule.
5. Prints league and team schedules.
6. Prints mailing labels for all coaches in a league.
7. Designed for use with League Standings using common data disk.

Each data disk handles:

26 teams per league.
Max. 50 leagues.

Single round robin (additional rounds can be created by rerunning the schedule).
Short-Term Reservations: Makes instant reservations for facilities with specific periods of availability (e.g., handball courts, practice fields).
Features:

1. Creates a weekly schedule for each facility with up to 12 time periods per day.
2. Reserves facilities up to 2 weeks in advance.
3. Prints facility schedule showing reserved time periods and contact persons.
4. Prints a reservation permit.

Each data disk handles 16 facilities.
Long-Term Reservations: Handles reservations when long lead times and variable-length time periods are desired.
Features:

1. Makes any number of reservations on specified date.
2. Reserves for any date or time in the future.
3. Reserves time periods with lengths of up to 99 days and up to 24 hours for each day.
4. Allows more than one organization to reserve facility at same time if desired.

5. Prints mailing labels for all contact persons of organizations reserving facilities.
6. Prints a reservation permit.
7. Records 2 categories of fees.

Each data disk handles:

1. 900 reservations
2. Max. 50 facilities
3. 600 organizations

League Registration: Organizes and provides easy access to league and player information.
Reports:

1. Team roster
2. League roster
3. Age report
4. Fee report
5. Resident report
6. Mailing labels

Capacity:

1. Program disk: 500 players in one or multiple leagues.
2. With additional data disk on a 2-drive system: 1100 players.
3. Additional data disks provide unlimited capacity.

Requires 1 or 2 disk drives.
$150.00

Baseball

Baseball Statistics

Win-loss record, game scores
Innings played
At bat
Hits (2B, 3B, HR)
Batting average
RBI's
On base

On base average
Sacrifices
Hits w/runner in scoring position
Batting average w/runners in scoring position
Slugging percentage
Stolen bases—caught stealing
Walks, strikeouts
Hit by pitch
Base on errors
Passed ball (catcher only)
Fielding:
  Putouts
  Assists
  Errors
  Fielding percentage
Pitching:
  Starter-reliever
  Complete game—save
  Win—loss—save
  Runs allowed
  Hits allowed
  Strikeouts—walks
  Hit batters
  Wild pitches
  Balks
  ERA
Ranks players by:
  Batting averages
  Fielding averages
  RBI's
Ranks pitchers by:
  ERA
  Win/loss record

$55.00

Slow Pitch

Same statistics as above with those not pertaining to slow-pitch
eliminated.
$45.00

Basketball

Basketball Statistics

Win/loss record, Scores by game/period
Quarters played, minutes played
Field goals attempted
Field goals made
Field goal percentage
Free throws attempted
Free throws made
Free throws percentage
Total points
Average points per game/period/minute
Offensive rebounds
Defensive rebounds
Fouls
Plus points—assists
   Steals and interceptions
   Loose ball recoveries
   Blocked shots
   Others (coaches choice)
Minus points—bad passes
   Fumbles
   Ballhandling errors
   Others (coaches choice)
Ranks players by:
   High scorer
   Field goal percentage
   Free throw percentage
   High rebounder
   Plus points total

$50.00

Ice Hockey

Ice Hockey Statistics

Win/loss record, scores by game/period
Power play shots on goal

Power play goals
Power play percentages
Short-handed shots on goal
Short-handed goals
Short-handed percentage
Assists
Total shots on goal
Total goals
Total goal percentage
Plus points (on ice when goal scored)
Minus points (on ice when opp. scored)
Minor penalties (# of minutes)
Major penalties (# of minutes)

Goalie Statistics:
   Minutes played
   Goals allowed
   Shots against (power play, short-handed, & totals)
   Average goals per game
   Save percentage
Penalties (minor/major)

$55.00

Soccer

Soccer Statistics

Periods played
Shots on goal
Goals scored
Goals percentage
Average goals per game
Assists (average per game)
Throw-ins attempted
Throw-ins good
Throw-ins percentage
Offsides (average)
Corner kicks attempted
Corner kicks good
Corner kicks percentage

Penalty kicks attempted
Penalty kicks good
Penalty kicks percentage
Fouls (direct kick result) (average)
Fouls (indirect kick result) (average)
Free kicks (direct kick) (average)
Free kicks (indirect kick) (average)

Goalie Statistics:
  Minutes played
  Shots against
  Saves
  Goals scored
  Save percentage
  Goal scored percentage
  Assists
  Average goals allowed per game (according to minutes played)

$50.00

Swimming

Swim Meet

Swim Meet is a management tool for competitive swimming events which:

1. Enters contestants in events
2. Assigns lanes in 6- or 8-lane pools
3. Prints heat sheets for either seeded preliminary or timed final events.

Other reports:

1. Contestants by event
2. Final standings

Each data disk handles:

1. 160 contestants
2. 32 events
3. 20 heats

Requires 2 disk drives
$145.00

Tennis

Tennis Draw

Tennis Draw is a computerized tournament management system which:

1. Registers players and teams in tournament events.
2. Creates a single-elimination random draw.
3. Seeds players and teams.
4. Follows USTA rules on byes and preliminary matches.

Capacity:

1. 8 to 64 players in 21 events simultaneously.

Requires 1 disk drive.
$60.00

Track and Field

Track and Field Statistics

All events
Times, places and points scored
Splits recorded
Records listed
Records broken—each meet
Top five individuals per event
Top ten individuals ranked—each meet
Indicates improvement

$45.00

Volleyball

Volleyball Statistics

Win-loss record, game/match scores
Games and matches played

Serves attempted
Serves good
Serve percentage
Ace serves
Ace serve percentage
Spikes attempted
Spikes good
Spiking percentage
Sets attempted
Sets good
Setting percentage
Serve receptions attempted
Serve receptions good
Receptions percentage
Blocks (individual & assists)
Point block (stuffs)
Blocking errors
Ball Handling errors
Violations (time, net, others)

$50.00

Apple II+ or later Apple model or Apple compatible computer of at least 48K. Printer of at least 70 columns required.

31. Micon Micro Systems
    P. O. Box 360
    Azle, TX 76020
    (817) 444-2533

Golf

Golf Handicap

Designed for golf club or country club or other organization requiring golf handicaps. This program maintains two files. One file, "names," contains the name of the golf club. The other file, "Golf 1," contains the members' names, their last 20 differentials, and the date they last played.

The handicap method agrees with the latest USGA Rules for determining handicaps. The program will hold more than 200 names, depending on the available memory. Theoretically, this program will hold up to 500 names. It has not been tested at that level.

The menu appears as follows:

1. For name additions
2. For update scores
3. For card print
4. For list handicaps
5. For screen list
6. For edit

Radio Shack TRS-80 Model II & III
48K 1 disk drive Printer not required
Model II $69.95 Plus $2.50 Postage & Handling
Model III $49.95 Plus $2.50 Postage & Handling

32. MicroScout
    680 Leeanne Ave.
    Yuba City, CA 95991
    (916) 671-7070

Basketball

HoopStat Basketball Statistics Program

Football

GridStat Football Statistics Program

Developed to run first on the Apple II+ and //e computer system
and second on the IBM.

33. Midwest Software
    Box 214
    Farmington, MI 48024
    (313) 477-0897

Basketball

Basketball Statistics

A menu-driven program written for the computer novice. If you
(or a student assistant) can turn on the machine and stick a disk in the
drive slot, you can use this program. It is completely error-trapped and
comes with excellent documentations to guide anyone gently through

the process of preparing complete statistics for a basketball team. The program allows you to enter a roster of up to 18 players, enter statistics for these players for up to 36 games per season, and effortlessly print out summaries for each game, season totals following each game, and the team's season record. Coaches who have used "Basketball Stats" report that it takes about 15 minutes to enter all statistics for a game and generate all hard copy summaries. To simplify the process of entering statistics, the program will generate a customized stat work sheet. Up to 15 statistics are supported by the program. Eleven statistics: 1. Quarters played, 2. Field goals made, 3. Field goals attempted, 4. Free throws made, 5. Free throws attempted, 6. Offensive rebounds, 7. Defensive rebounds, 8. Turnovers, 9. Assists, 10. Steals, 11. Blocked shots are all built in. You may define up to 4 additional statistics for added flexibility. Total points, shooting percentages, total rebounds, games played and game averages for all statistics are generated by the computer. Files are disk-based for speed and reliability. Separate files are maintained for each game allowing you to review any game or print a game summary at any time. All the files for an entire season easily fit into a single disk for efficient storage.

Additional features include a full corrections routine for all entries, and ability to add players at any time, the handling of up to 4 overtime periods per game, and personalized reports for your school, season or coach. "Basketball Stats" is compiled for high speed of execution and complete reliability.

Apple II+ & Apple //e
Commodore 64 32K Pet
$39.50

34. Misc Inc.
1530 Butternut Circle
Gastonia, NC 28052
(704) 865-7177

Swimming

Swim Meet Seeding And Official Results-SM40

Does everything required for any swim meet. Produces labels for cards and awards. Prints prelims and final heat sheets. Produces final official results.

This program was written by trained swimming officials and is designed to have the flexibility to handle any swim meet including the nationals. Every normal swimming situation and most unusual ones can be handled by this program. Using a minimum of manpower involved with scoring and administration, this program will allow you to run a good meet with results being posted quickly and accurately. With this system a chief scorer, an assistant scorer, a computer operator and an awards clerk should be able to handle the administrative functions of any meet. The clerk of the course and a computer typist should be able to prepare a large heat sheet in just a few hours of work plus printing time.

The program is menu driven and contains 17 programs and over 100K of code. The program works with any size pool from 2 to 10 lanes in meters or yards. Error correction routines are supplied throughout to correct operator errors.

Main Menu SM40

Select option desired:

1. Prepare order of events
2. Enter swimmers
3. Print list of entries (psych sheet)
4. Send entries
5. Print labels
6. Score
7. Correct files
8. Compute points scored
9. Paginate heat sheet or final results
10. Prepare entry forms
11. Inquiry
    Exit

Correction Menu SM40
Select one:

1. Change order of events
2. Change time record names
3. Change swimmer's name or club
4. Add swimmers
5. Delete swimmers
6. Re-seed event
7. Change recorded results
8. Print list of entries for re-seed event

9. Change number of lanes
10. Merge entries/separate results
    Exit

Radio Shack TRS-80 Level II Model I or III
32K or more of memory—2 disk drives
80 column or more printer is required
The program is being converted to Apple II and the IBM PC
$250.00 for TRS-80
$275.00 for Apple and IBM
Add $2.00 for postage

35. Performance Management Assoc.
    501 S. Kinney
    Mt. Pleasant, MI 48858

Football

Quarterback Performance

This computer model of quarterback performance allows a coach to evaluate a prospective QB in 17 performance areas (e.g., running speed, passing ability, stress tolerance) and then receive instant feedback on predicted game performance (rushing and passing statistics) for the entire season. The system can be used to determine quarterback selection, strengths and weaknesses, how he fits with a given offensive strategy, and areas for improvement. The software package is compatable with a number of micro-computers.

36. Practi-Ware
    P. O. Box 1216
    Talladega, AL 35160

Baseball

Baseball Statistics

Baseball Statistics has been designed as a low-cost, simple-to-use, time-efficient software package. The system will let the coach know what he needs to know about his players.

In using the program, you simply enter the statistics from each game into the computer. For a team of about 20 players this takes no longer than ten minutes. The computer does the rest of the work. It provides you with three different printouts: team statistics per game, team totals thus far, and individual statistics per game and total.

The software runs on an Apple //e with a printer.

Price $65.00.

Practi-Ware is also planning to market several other athletic programs in the future. These include football tendency/scouting reports, football statistics, and weight training. If you have some other need, they will be happy to set up a personalized program for your athletic ventures.

37. R & R Software
7016 Canevalley Circle
Citrus Heights, CA 95610
(916) 728-5047

R & R's Sport Pak consists of four tape cassette programs designed to save, retrieve and display sport statistics. The four programs include Baseball/Softball Team Statistics, Baseball Pitcher Statistics, Football Team Statistics and Track Meet Statistics. All four programs are on one tape.

Baseball

Baseball/Softball Team Statistics

Complete scorebook-oriented program for storing and displaying 10 of the most common individual and team statistics (AB's, hits, batting average, etc.). Team totals automatically computed. Cumulative season totals easy to compute.

Baseball Pitcher Statistics: Allows you to keep 12 statistics on each of your pitchers, such as total innings pitched, total earned runs, total walks, balks, etc. The program allows cumulative season or any combination of game statistics previously saved to be accumulated and either saved or displayed.

Football

Football Team Statistics

Three programs in one: defense, defense and special teams. 38 different types of statistics stored, displayed and computed. Graphics included.

Track and Field

Track Meet Statistics

Names, times and schools of the 1st, 2nd, and 3rd place winners are input to give total team points at any time. Covers yards or meters for 15 of the most common dual track meet events. For use during or after meet.

Radio Shack Min Req Mod 3 - 16K
Cassette only $29.95

38. Rainbow Computing, Inc.
9719 Reseda Blvd.
Northridge, CA 91324
(213) 349-5560

Baseball

Bat-Stat

Bat-Stat is designed to keep track of cumulative batting statistics for a baseball team of up to 20 players. Player statistics and team totals are given for both current game and season. Ten statistical categories are provided: At Bats, Runs, Hits, Batting Average, Doubles, Triples, Home Runs, Sacrifices, Walks, and Runs Batted In. Batting averages are automatically computed. Bat-State features: easy data entry and editing, error-handling, team roster listing, blank score sheet printing, and game and season report printing.

Apple II+ or Apple //e, Disk Drive, 80-column printer.
Retail Price: Disk $49.95.

Bowling

Bowling Data System

A program for bowling leagues that provides accurate record-keeping and report generation. For leagues up to 40 teams with up to six bowlers per team. It allows a league secretary to customize all pertinent parameters. A cumulative record is kept of total pins, games won and lost, total points, high series and so forth for each team. It also maintains high game, handicap, and other data as needed.

Weekly scores for each bowler are entered from score sheets provided by the system. It then prints a weekly recap report and the scope sheets to be used for the following week, as well as generating team and lane pairings. A season average report is also produced listing all bowlers in the league in descending order by average.

Apple
80 column printer required

39. Rick Stellfox
    264 East McMurray Road
    McMurray, Pennsylvania 15317

Basketball

Basketball Stats

With this program you can:

1. Enter team roster and add names at any time.
2. Enter game stats.
3. Calculate cumulative stats.
4. Calculate average stats.
5. Print all stats in chart form.
6. Print individual stats for any player.
7. Print specific stats ranked from highest to lowest for cumulative and average data.
8. Save cumulative stats on diskette.
9. Call back stats from diskette.
10. Edit data:
    Change items in the file.
    Correct spelling of names.
    Scratch player from roster/keep data.

TRS-80 Model III.
Price: $25.00
Baseball program will be available in the future.

40. RMV Programs and Consulting
    Rick VanSickle
    P. O. Box 341
    Aztec, NM 87410
    (505) 334-6445

Baseball

Baseball Statistics

Baseball Statistics include:

At Bat	Strikeouts
Runs	Putouts

Hits   Assists
2B Hits   Errors
3B Hits   Field Pct.
Homeruns   Bat Avg.
Walks

Pitching Statistics include:
Games   Walks
Runs   Won
Earned Runs   Lost
Innings Pitched   Saves
Strikeouts   ERA

Basketball

Basketball Statistics

FG Made   Turn Overs
FG Att.   Turn Over Avg.
FG Pct.   Asst.
FT Made   Asst. Avg.
FT Att.   Steals
FT Pct.   Steal Avg.
Total Pts.   Rebounds Off Total
Pt. Avg.   Rebounds Def Total
Min. Played   Rebounds Game Avg.
Fouls

Apple
Baseball, Basketball combination sell for $25.00.

41. Schuh, R. L.
    4321 S. 37th St.
    St. Louis, MO 63116
    (314) 351-6606

Baseball

Baseball/Softball Statistics

The system maintains and prints player and team statistics for a baseball/softball league. (It can also be used for corkball, fuzzball, and other games derived from baseball).

Player information includes:

Name and telephone number
Games played
Hitting
  At bat
  Hits
  2 base hits
  3 base hits
  Home runs
  Walks
  Outs
Pitching
  Games
  Won
  Lost
  Runs
  Earned runs
  Hits
  Walks
  Strikeouts
  Home runs
  Innings pitched
Team data includes:
  Name
  Manager and phone number
  Games
    Won-lost
  Runs scored
    Allowed
League record contains:
  League name
  Secretary and phone number

Statistics show:

1. Team standings
   Games won, lost and percentages
   Runs scored
   Runs allowed

2. Individual leaders—hitting
    Batting average
    Runs scored
    Home runs
    Runs batted in
    Total bases
    On base average
    Slugging percentage
3. Individual leaders—pitching
    Games won—lost and percentage
    Earned run averages

Team statistics include:

Games won—lost and percentage

Individual records show:

Hitting
    Games
    At bat
    Hits
    Average
    Runs
    Runs batted in
    Home runs
    2 base hits
    3 base hits
    Walks
    Strikeouts
Pitching
    Games
    Won—lost and percentage
    Runs
    Earned runs
    Hits
    Walks
    Strikeouts
    Innings pitched

Golf

Golf League Statistics

The system maintains and prints player and team statistics for a golf league.

Player information includes:

Player's name and telephone number
Total handicap differential
Number of rounds posted by system
Number of rounds used in computing handicap
Player's current handicap
Player's low gross score
Player's low net score
Number of points earned last round
Total number of points earned
Date of player's last round
Hole-by-hole score and total strokes for the round

Team data includes:

Team name
Team points last round
Team total points

Up to 26 golf courses may be used by a league. Golf course data is entered to the system by the user and includes:

Golf course name
Number of holes on the course
Par for number of holes played
USGA rating for the course
Starting hole

Two programs comprise the system:

Golf 3 File Maintenance
    Adds or deletes records to the file
    Posts player and team data
    File maintenance:

Adds 3 types of records
League record
Golf course record
Team record
Deletes 4 types of records
League record
Golf course record
Team record
Player's record

Golf 4 Prints The League Statistics
The listing is sequenced by team
When all teams are listed, team standings are printed
Individual high point average, low net, and low net for the week, are also printed. Systems are priced at $50.00 each.

42. Sherman House
16 Abbot Street
Andover, MA 01810

Player Ratings

Athletic Rating Program

Allows you to analyze the qualifications for success in any sport you choose, and then to assess the capabilities of your athletes to perform according to these qualifications. Properly used, the program will assist you in selecting a team ("cutting"); it will identify areas of strength and weakness in individual players; it will check the development of the players as the season progresses; and will provide an indication of the effectiveness of your coaching in various aspects of the sport.

A unique, tested program selects top prospects, highlights for improvement, adaptable to any sport; no computer knowledge necessary; simple to use. Presently used for *football, soccer, basketball* and *lacrosse*.

Apple II Disk $24.95
Radio Shack TRS-80 Mod I & II Tape $16.95
Commodore Vic or 64 Tape $16.95
Listing of basic code $3.50
16K recommended but will run on less
Program written by Paul Kalkstein

43. Soft-Mix Enterprises
    737 North Governor Road
    Valparaiso, IN 46383
    (219) 759-3667

Football

Football Statistics

Program 1—Lets you enter your team's numbers and names as well as your opponents' teams' numbers and names and saves them in a sequential file for later use.

Program 2—Is a sequential file for the variables used in the Main Program. This program is already set up on the diskette ready for use.

Program 3—Is the Main Program. It lets you input a play-by-play description of the game by asking you questions that are answered YES or NO, by inputting players involved in a play by entering their JERSEY numbers and by asking you to input the yard line ball is marked, so computer can figure out the yards gained or lost on a particular play. This program covers:

 1. Kickoffs
 2. Kickoff Returns
 3. Running Plays
 4. Passing Plays
 5. Punts
 6. Punt Returns
 7. Penalties
 8. Fumbles
 9. Pass Interceptions
10. Other Scoring
11. Game Statistics By Quarter
12. Individual Statistics

Program 4—Allows for the printout of all individual stats for the hometeam.

Program 5—Allows for the printout of all individual stats for the opponents.

Program 6—Is actually a set of 4 programs that will allow you to make computer operator corrections to any of the previously mentioned catagories for either team.

Program 7—Is actually a set of 10 programs that will allow you to get individual stats for the home team and totals for the opponents for any number of games or at the end of the season.

Program 8—Is a maintenance program that allows you to make adjustments in the player data file, such as number changes, addition and/or deletions of players from the roster.

All printouts are on a 8.5 × 11 sheet of paper.

These programs are available on any Commodore computer and the Apple II computer with a minimum of 32K.

The cost of this package is $200.00

44. Software Associates of North East
    P. O. Box 70
    North East, PA 16428
    (814) 725-9279 or (814) 725-5308

Football

Quik Stat

Gives you team and individual statistics for a single game and an entire season.

Accurate statistics are:

An evaluation of your team's performance as well as your opponents'.

A means of establishing good communications with the media and the community and your team.

An incentive for improved team performance.

The Quick Stat printout gives team and individual statistics in the following areas:

Rushing	Kickoff Returns
Passing	Punt Returns
Receiving	Punts
Scoring	Kickoffs
Total Yards	Field Goals
Fumbles	Penalties
Interceptions	First Downs

To use the Quik Stat program the following hardware is needed:
    Any Apple Computer System with 48K

One or two Apple Disk Drives
One printer, capable of printing 80 characters per line

Price: $100.00

45. Sports Data Services
    P. O. Box 12268
    St. Paul, MN 55112
    (612) 571-4892

Sports Data Services has developed a complete line of software programs for the purpose of calculating athletic statistics on the micro-computer. Each diskette is fully programmed, with easy-to-follow on-screen instructions, designed for those with no prior experience on a micro-computer.

Sports statistic programs available from Sports Data Services:

Baseball
Basketball
Hockey
Track and Field
Volleyball
Soccer
Softball (Fast and Slow Pitch)
Gymnastics
Swimming
Football

Sports Data Services statistics programs will compute:

Game scores
Scores by period, inning or quarter
Overall win/loss record
Conference win/loss record
Non-conference statistics
Individual single game statistics
Team single game statistics
Individual cumulative statistics
Team cumulative statistics
Individual per-game averages
Team per-game averages

All Sports Data Services Programs calculate statistics for the team as well as individual participants. Statistics entered for each individual after each game will generate your team statistics for each game as well as cumulative statistics, which can be referenced at any time. These programs complete your statistics in minutes, with complete accuracy, enabling you to have important information in a fraction of the time you are now spending.

With each program you receive:

1. Software disk with ready-to-use statistics program.
2. Complete easy-to-understand documentation manual.
3. Statistic sheets for easy data entry and transfer.
4. 90 day money-back guarantee against defects in materials or workmanship.

Currently, the programs are written in Apple Soft Basic and require an Apple or Apple compatible computer of at least 48K and 1 disc drive. Require 80-column printer.

Price range $45.00 to $55.00 plus $3.00 Postage/Handling. Buy one Sports Data Services statistic program and purchase any additional programs for 10% off.

46. Sports Log
    27 Broadaxe Lane
    Wilton, CT 06897
    (203) 834-1750

Athletic Administration

Sports Log

Sports Log handles all aspects of the administration of sports programs including player registration, team formation, league scheduling and league standings. Sports Log will also prepare checks to pay officials. Complete accounting of program revenues and expenses is available with the Plus version. Round-robin and elimination schedules are quickly prepared. Matches may be assigned to available resources (fields, courts, etc.) and officials assigned to scheduled matches. Resource usage may be monitored and tracked. League standings are maintained according to user-specified criteria.

Sports Log is available in four versions:

1. Standard Log.
   Performs all functions except complete accounting of program revenues and expenses.
2. Log Plus.
   Does everything. Accounts for program revenues and expenses. Slightly more sophisticated scheduling routines.
3. Basic Log.
   Includes the routines necessary to administer a sports program. Excludes certain sophisticated and custom routines.
4. Log Scheduler.
   The Standard Log without the player data files and associated routines.

The Sports Log system runs on any computer which has an MS-DOS, CP/M or UNIX operating system. Sports Log systems are specifically tailored to your equipment—the system is supplied as a single diskette or multiple diskettes, depending upon the storage capacity of the diskettes for your system. All Sports Log systems are menu driven for easy use.

47. Sports Medical Technology Corp.
    P. O. Box 656
    Center Moriches, NY 11934
    (516) 878-0101

Conditioning

Performance 2000

Performance 2000 is a computerized fitness evaluation system designed for use in a non-medical setting. The subject is paced through a submaximal routine, and the computer records and analyzes the physiological responses. Performance 2000 establishes a norm, determines present condition, suggests an exercise plan, and tracks the progress to improve present condition and reach the norm. It will determine present level of fitness, suggest exercise plans and evaluate progress in training.

Performance 2000 was designed for trainers, colleges, clinics, coaches, high schools, screening centers, health clubs, spas, and sports clubs; in short, any individual or organization concerned with assessing and developing fitness, health, safety and productivity.

48. Sports Training Systems
    4255 Sandalwood Cir.
    Nacogdoches, TX 75961
    (409) 560-2138

Track and Field

Sports Training and Systems

The Track & Field Package will greatly enhance your potential for developing systematic track and field workouts and evaluation procedures. With this system, athlete and coach are able to monitor several different areas of athletic accomplishment based on goal-setting and periodic testing.

This software package is designed to be a guideline in reaching athletic goals. Remember that the computer is a machine and cannot know when the athlete is tired or injured. Also the computer does not make any allowances for environmental changes. If the athlete has problems in following the paces prescribed for him then careful evaluation of the athlete is essential before continuing. The computer only supplies basic information that is available to the coach. It does not predict how many repetitions—how far the training distances are—or how much rest the coach allows the athlete to take. Therefore, the system is dependent on the creativity and flexibility of the coach.

Program Description:

GOLSET—designed to project workout times week by week, determined from goals and time trail evaluation.

TOTAL PRO—This program is almost identical to GOLSET. However, it will calculate split times or workout times for various distances. It is a very long program if done over a period of several weeks. Other programs (MPS) in the system are designed to give you the same information on a daily basis as compared to total weekly workouts.

MPS—This program is designed to give the coach workout times for any distance desired based on meters per second evaluation derived from GOLSET or TOTAL PRO.

EXTIN—This program is designed to evaluate athlete progress in workouts. It helps the athlete and coach analyze his/her workload and compare results to coach's projection for that session.

SPLIT—This program is designed to calculate split times from total stopwatch splits. Can be used as evaluation of uniformity of race pace or training pace.

STEPDOWN—This program is designed to calculate meters per second for distances that are used in evaluation. Workouts that are stepdown or stepup in nature can be evaluated to see if even pace is achieved or if uneven pace is desired.

ANSPRINT—This program is designed to calculate sprinter-oriented workouts. It averages total repetitions and compares it to projected goals. It then calculates new workloads for that athlete.

FIELD EVENT—This program is designed to average field event performances in feet and inches. It also places emphasis on fouls to keep athlete aware of a mistake in that area.

HORIZONTAL ANALYSIS—This program is designed to average horizonal jump distances and incorporate runway time. Helps the athlete and coach to compare times to distances obtained.

THROWS ANALYSIS—This program is designed to show a comparison between standing throws and full technique throws. It is used to determine if technique is inferior to strength.

PROWORK—This program is designed to print out daily workout schedules based on a number system. It is basically a word processor and helps keep accurate and neat records. It can be used to individualize workout schedules or used as a group schedule.

WEIGHT TRAINING—This program is designed to develop a six-week or 18-day weight training program. It is used to help the athlete reach 105 percent of the maximum tested prior to implementation.

Sports Training Systems include:

System 1—Goal-Setting and Projection of Times for Workouts and Competition. 800 Meters to 10,000.

System 2—Workout Analysis and Performance Analysis. 100 to 10,000 Meters.

System 3—Field Event Analysis and Horizontal Jumps and Throws.

System 4—Weight Training and Six Week Program.

Prices: System 1 $59.95
         System 2 $49.95
         System 3 $29.95
         System 4 $29.95
Packages Prices: System 1 & 2 $89.95
                  System 1, 2 & 3 $99.95
                  Total System $119.95

49. Sterling Swift Publishing Company
   7901 South IH-35
   Austin, TX 78744
   (512) 282-6840

Football

Computer-Enhanced Football Training presents 50 Defense vs. Run

This program is "user friendly," menu driven, and no prior computer experience is necessary.

You get two floppy disks plus one Coaching Manual—for interactive player learning.

This package contains six lessons with animated and static graphics:

1. Defensive Goals
2. Principles
3. End Play
4. Perimeter Play
5. Linebacker Play
6. Down Lineman Play

50 Defense vs. Run is the first of a family of football products dealing with the mental side of football. Forthcoming products will include:

1. 50 Defense vs Pass
2. Offense (Run)
3. Offense (Pass)
4. Kicking (Offense/Defense)

CEFT can be used one-on-one to allow for varied learning rates, or with specific groups such as ends, backs, linemen, linebackers, defensive backs, or with the complete team (using a large screen projector).

Other CEFT programs now available are:
   50 Defense vs Pass
   Kicking—Offense/Defense

Hardware Required
   Apple II Plus or //e
   Monitor

Single Disk Drive
48K, DOS 3.3
50 Defense vs Run (Includes two disks plus manual) $99.95
Subsequent sets purchased and billed to same school account
$49.98
Shipping/Handling per set $2.00
Hands-on Preview Disk (refundable on purchase of a package)
$9.95
Shipping/Handling per disk $1.00
Program written by Frank Downing, Ralph Heimer and Tim
Robinson

50. The Winning Edge
    P. O. Box 77383-1944
    Spring, TX 77383
    (713) 353-1777 (after 5 p.m.)

Administration
Recruiting

Sells CHAMPS athletic software. See 10 above.

51. TIES
    1925 West Country Road B2
    Saint Paul, MN 55113
    (612) 638-2348

Basketball/Softball
Basketball
Bowling
Football
Hockey
Soccer
Volleyball
Wrestling

Sports Stats

Sports Stats allows users to process athletic statistical data for
individual and/or team performance. Users may choose from 14 available routines for basketball, wrestling, hockey, baseball/softball, football, volleyball, soccer, and bowling. Statistical data is generated for
each game and/or player, and may be accumulated over the season.

The input for each of the routines varies depending on the nature of the sport; however, all routines in Sports Stats use data stored in files. These files contain either players' names or statistical data. The routines and data from these files may be used to generate reports. A typical user might enter current data from a recent athletic event, produce a statistical report, and then update the data by saving it in the permanent file. As the season progresses, reports made from the permanent file would thus show accumulated data and the corresponding statistics.

Hardware needed: 48K Apple II, or Apple //e, with Applesoft BASIC, DOS 3.3, Autostart, one-disk drive, and monitor. This package is designed to work with printers that connect to an Apple communications, serial, super serial, or parallel card. It will also work with a Malibu 165 card, a CCS serial card, or a Grappler card.

Price: $50.00.

INDEX

USING THE PERSONAL COMPUTER FOR OFFENSIVE FOOTBALL SCOUTING
The New Competitive Edge

Alan B. Hatfield & Charles S. Frazier

Coaches from the NFL to the high school level are now taking advantage of a *new competitive edge*: the use of a personal computer to analyze football scouting reports.

This innovative handbook covers every aspect of the *new competitive edge* and shows you how to use a PC to compile, analyze, summarize, store, display and print-out the valuable scouting information you need to tailor a winning game plan against each opponent you face.

The best part is that no previous computer experience is necessary! *In less than an hour* you will be able to prepare a sophisticated scouting report that would normally take several coaches many long, hard hours to prepare.

Written in clear, down-to-earth language, the handbook spells out each simple step, and provides you with dozens of helpful charts, forms, schedules, vivid examples—plus fully illustrated instructions.

To start, you get specific guidelines that make it easy for you to select the right personal computer system to meet your particular needs—and budget. Plus, you'll find a comprehensive software directory that helps you choose from among the high-quality football scouting programs available today.